LAW OF THE LAND

A Practical Legal Guide for Tourists and Business Travelers

Brazil

By Michael L. Moore Esq.

Edited by Ally Knez-Siddique

Cover Design: Kristina Conatser

Published by: Law of the Land Publishing LLC

ISBN: 978-1-964870-08-3

DEDICATION

This book is dedicated to the memory of my late older brother, Kenneth Lee Moore, whose tragic murder at 15 years of age inspired me to write this series of books.

This book is also dedicated to my parents, John Henry Moore, and Edna Mae Moore, whose tremendous parenting skills kept me focused on the important things in life: being reverent, getting educated, and prioritizing family.

Finally, this book is dedicated to my beautiful family, my wife Royellen, my son AJ, and my daughter Karla. They inspire me every single day to be kind, patient, and compassionate.

IN LOVING MEMORY OF:

Belinda Joyce Moore Moss—my beautiful and wonderful sister, who supported me in every positive thing that I ever attempted to do.

Michael Eugene Baker—my dedicated and loyal friend and brother, who always wanted the very best for me.

Sylvia Joyce Hill—my eldest sister, who had a beautiful spirit and was like a second mother to me.

LAW OF THE LAND

PUBLISHING for Tourists & Business Travelers

Travel smart. Stay legal. Stay safe.®

From local laws to medical guides we've got you covered world wide
in one digital platform.

Travel Safe Anywhere
3 MONTHS FREE TRIAL

SCAN QR code
for more info

PREFACE

My introduction to the justice system came when I was only 10 years old. My 15-year-old brother was murdered with a butcher knife by a 19-year-old in a simple argument over a torn shirt. I was devastated by his death and sought retribution for his fate that never came. The woman was initially charged with second degree murder, but after plea negotiations, she was convicted of manslaughter and sentenced to only five years in a youthful offender school and ordered to undergo psychiatric care. That was it. Nothing more. The judicial system had run its course.

My family knew nothing about the justice system, and we did not have the tools to advocate for ourselves. No one provided us with a written source to reference for guidance through this process. There was no easily accessible, easy to understand, definitive source to educate ourselves about the legal system that we suddenly and unexpectedly found ourselves immersed in after being victimized by such a violent criminal act.

As I got older, finished college, law school, and ultimately started practicing law, it became clear to me that most people are not knowledgeable about the law or how the judicial process works. If most people are uninformed here in the United States regarding the law and the legal process, how would they fare when in other countries? I realized that tourists and businesspeople who travel internationally needed access to information on how to navigate the legal system in other countries!

For many years, there has been considerable media attention focused on international travelers experiencing legal difficulties while traveling abroad. Most of these news stories gained attention in the United States and abroad because they involved American citizens facing punishment that was considered "unconventional" and "harsh" by United States' legal standards. I recall a news story in 1994 regarding Michael Fay, a young American male, who had broken the law in Singapore. He was convicted and sentenced to be caned and or whipped publicly. While the United States Government weighed in on the inappropriate and cruel nature of the punishment, the young American was beaten because he had been convicted under Singapore law.

Similarly, in recent years, international news stories have garnered headlines regarding foreign travelers and their issues with the laws of countries that were not their own. Amanda Knox, an American woman, was accused of murdering her roommate in Italy in 2007 and spent almost four years in an Italian prison before being definitively acquitted by the Supreme Court of Cassatio. Kenneth Bae, an American citizen, was arrested in North Korea in 2012 and was convicted for hostile acts against the communist country. He was sentenced to 15 years hard labor but was released in 2014 after efforts by the U.S. State Department. More recently, United States Basketball Star, Brittany Griner was arrested in February 2022 at a Moscow airport on drug-related charges and detained for nearly 10 months, spending much of that time in prison. Her plight unfolded at the same time Russia invaded Ukraine and further heightened tensions between Russia and the United States, ending only after she was freed in exchange for a notorious Russian arms dealer.

It was in 1994 that another personal tragic event occurred that finally inspired me to write these series of books. A dear friend and also client of mine was brutally murdered while on his second honeymoon in Jamaica. News of his murder shocked me and our local community. The legal hurdles his family had to overcome to see that justice was properly dispensed far away from home, in another country, with an entirely different set of criminal procedural rules and laws, was difficult to navigate.

As I was my friend's attorney at the time of his death, his family asked that I act as their "legal liaison" to the Jamaican Prosecutor's Office and to the Jamaican Police Department. I participated in multiple police interviews with my client's widow because she was the primary witness to his murder. As a former prosecuting attorney, I was also allowed by the Court, as a professional courtesy, to sit at the prosecutor's table to consult with the prosecuting attorney during trial. What I observed about the Jamaican trial process from a front row seat was compelling enough to cause me to seriously consider educating the "world" regarding what to expect and how to act appropriately when faced with legal issues while traveling abroad.

One of the realities in life is that, regardless of what country you are in, it is never a pleasant experience to run afoul of the law and be forced to accept that someone else will be making a decision about your pecuniary, proprietary, or penal interests (your money, your property, or your freedom).

It is important to know what the laws are, how they apply to you, and how to navigate the legal system if you are charged with a crime. It is also very helpful to know what resources are available to you if you are the victim of a criminal act. At the end of the day, an "ounce of prevention is worth a pound of cure," so the more knowledge you have, the more ammunition you possess, and the more likely you will have a positive outcome.

If you are traveling to Brazil, the first thing you should pack is a copy of this book! The helpful information and tips contained in this volume will provide a great starting point for knowing what to do (and not to do!) when you arrive at your destination and will help ensure that you have a wonderful vacation or business trip unmarred by tangles with the law.

TABLE OF CONTENTS

INTRODUCTION

INTRODUCTION

As a practicing attorney for over 34 years, I have encountered numerous clients who travel often, but are unaware of the laws of the land they are traveling to.

Therefore, many years ago, I decided to write a series of books that would explain the laws of specific countries. My focus was to explain the laws that may affect travelers in a straightforward manner, without all of the legal language that is sometimes hard for even seasoned attorneys to understand.

About This Book

The aim of this book is simple. It provides you, the traveler, with a simple, easy to read book that will provide a basic legal guide that explains the law in the country that you are about to visit. It is not intended to educate you on ALL of the laws in a given country. The goal is to provide you with the details of the most common legal and safety issues faced by tourists and business travelers.

I have also provided context with background information on places not to visit, statistics on the country and prevention measures you should take to safeguard your legal and physical safety. Knowledge is a powerful thing and knowing how to stay out of trouble (or how to get out of it!) is important for everyone who travels.

This *Law of The Land/Brazil* book simply helps you become more informed about your legal rights, responsibilities, and obligations in a wide range of subject areas.

Last, but not least, this book does NOT purport to offer legal advice. It does, however, provide the information you need to stay safe, follow the law and navigate around legal difficulties. However, if you do face legal difficulties, the information in this book will provide you with a starting point for solving the problem and obtaining legal assistance should it be required.

Hypotheticals Used Throughout This Book

From time to time throughout this book, I will explain the law to readers by using hypothetical scenarios. These hypotheticals will be marked by an icon that will be explained in further detail as you read on.

How This Book is Organized

CHAPTER 1: **About Brazil.** This chapter will provide you with a brief overview about Brazil and its history. It also addresses Visa requirements, monetary advice, and the best times to visit.

CHAPTER 2: **Customs.** This chapter will provide information on what to expect when entering Brazil. It will also explain what restricted and prohibited items are when entering Brazil along with custom's regulations.

CHAPTER 3: **Crime in Brazil.** This chapter provides an overview of the history of crime in Brazil and steps that Brazilian officials have taken to curb the high rate of crime.

CHAPTER 4: **Criminal Law Violations.** This chapter will provide information on drug offenses, penalties, true events and questions and answers.

CHAPTER 5: **Alcohol-Related Offenses.** This chapter will provide key points regarding the sale, consumption, and regulations of alcohol use in Brazil.

CHAPTER 6: **Firearm & Ammunition Offenses.** This chapter will provide key points regarding the possession of firearms and ammunition in Brazil.

CHAPTER 7: **Prostitution.** This chapter provides an overview of the history of prostitution in Brazil, laws and penalties, prostitution practices, sex trafficking, sex tourism, health in Brazil, tips to avoid being hassled, a Law of the Land Hypothetical, and the current situation on prostitution in Brazil.

CHAPTER 8: **LGBTQ.** This chapter will provide information regarding the acceptance of LGBTQ people in Brazil, and the laws surrounding homosexuality.

CHAPTER 9: **Sexually Motivated/Violent Crimes.** This chapter will provide an overview of sexually related crimes in Brazil.

CHAPTER 10: **Arrested in Brazil.** This chapter will provide information on what to do if you are arrested in Brazil.

CHAPTER 11: **Jails vs. Prisons: Conditions & Culture.** This chapter will provide information on the conditions and culture of Brazilian jails and prisons.

CHAPTER 12: **Helping a Friend or Relative Imprisoned in Brazil.** This chapter will provide information on how you can assist a friend or relative imprisoned in Brazil.

CHAPTER 13: **The Administration of Justice.** This chapter will provide information on Brazil's Judicial System.

CHAPTER 14: **Crime Victim Assistance.** This chapter will provide information on crime victim assistance along with providing safety tips.

CHAPTER 15: **Police.** This chapter will provide information on the Brazilian Police and how to report a crime.

CHAPTER 16: **How to Get Legal Help in Brazil.** This chapter will provide information regarding how to obtain legal assistance for travelers to Brazil.

CHAPTER 17: **Medical Facilities & Hospitals.** This chapter will provide information about how to obtain medical care while visiting Brazil.

CHAPTER 18: **Driving in Brazil.** This chapter will provide information on driving in Brazil, traffic rules, and road safety tips.

CHAPTER 19: **Nude Beaches and Clothing-Optional Resorts.** This chapter will provide an overview of nude beaches and resorts in Brazil, and the legality and safety of visiting nude beaches.

CHAPTER 20: **Unusual Laws.** This chapter will provide information on some unusual laws in Brazil, and related penalties and fines.

CHAPTER 21: **Traveling Safely.** This chapter will provide some crime prevention information when traveling solo, traveling as a family, and generally when traveling for all travelers.

CHAPTER 22: **Tourist Taxation.** This chapter will provide information on taxes that tourists are required to pay in Brazil.

CHAPTER 23: **Long-Term Stays.** This chapter will provide an overview of the consequences for overstaying your visit to Brazil.

CHAPTER 24: **Civil Litigation.** This chapter will provide information about the civil litigation process in Brazil.

CHAPTER 25: **Other Things to Know.** This chapter will provide information on the harassment of tourists, travel and safety, and other practical tips.

CHAPTER 26: **Quick Reference Guide.** This chapter is a quick way to get information. It is a condensed version of the chapters in this book.

Emergency/Important Contact Numbers in Brazil

Useful Portuguese Phrases

Glossary

Icons Used in this Book

What do those pictures throughout the book mean? See below:

 WARNING: This icon flags information about things you should **avoid** while visiting Brazil. Heed the advice next to this icon to avoid legal perils.

 REMEMBER: This icon flags noteworthy information that you **shouldn't forget.**

 HELPFUL TIPS: This icon flags information that will help you when entering Brazil, relates to a legal situation, or refers to resources available while visiting Brazil.

 TECHNICAL INFORMATION: This icon flags technical aspects of the law. If you are faced with a legal problem, and you want to learn more about the law involved, this information can be helpful.

 **ADDITIONAL INFORMATION**: This icon points to the location of additional information available on the internet.

 **HYPOTHETICAL**: This icon points to hypothetical scenarios to illustrate possible legal problems and the outcome.

 **QUESTIONS**: This icon points to questions and answers throughout the book.

 **TRUE STORY**: This icon points to true events throughout the book.

Where to Go From Here

If you have a specific question about the law in Brazil as it relates to a specific area, just turn to the chapter that addresses that issue, or turn to the Quick Reference Guide.

You can also read the book from cover to cover to obtain a more comprehensive understanding of the Brazilian laws and resources available should you find yourself in a legal predicament while visiting.

 **Disclaimer:** While the recommendations in this book primarily address U.S. citizens, the information is relevant and applicable to citizens of any country.

CHAPTER 1
ABOUT BRAZIL

ABOUT BRAZIL

About Brazil[1]

Brazil, officially known as the Federal Republic of Brazil, is the largest country in South America, and the fifth most populated nation in the entire world, with a population of approximately 215 million people, according to the most recent estimates. The capital of Brazil, Brasília, was deliberately established in the country's center to facilitate better connectivity between different regions and promote economic development across the nation. Brazil is a vast country and shares a border with every country in South America, except Ecuador and Chile. From north to south and from east to west, Brazil spans nearly 2,700 miles and forms a massive irregular triangle.

Brazil is divided into five large geographic and statistical units called the "Major Regions" (*Grandes Regiões*): North (*Norte*), Northeast (*Nordeste*), Central-West (*Centro-Oeste*), Southeast (*Sudeste*), and South (*Sur*). The country is home to a variety of tropical and subtropical landscapes that include plateaus, low mountains, savannas, and wetlands. Most of the Amazon River basin, which has the world's largest river system and most extensive virgin rainforest, is also contained within Brazil.

Brazil is most famous for its vibrant Carnival, the world's largest festival, celebrated with samba music, colorful parades, and elaborate

---

1   https://www.britannica.com/place/Brazil

costumes, especially in Rio de Janeiro. The country is also renowned for the Amazon Rainforest, the largest tropical rainforest on Earth, which is vital for global biodiversity and climate. Brazil is a football (soccer) powerhouse, having won the FIFA World Cup five times, with legendary players like Pelé and Neymar. Additionally, the iconic Christ the Redeemer statue in Rio de Janeiro, one of the New Seven Wonders of the World, stands as a symbol of Brazil's cultural and religious identity.

Brief History of Brazil[2]

The area now known as Brazil has been inhabited since around 9000 BCE, originally by indigenous peoples. European explorers first arrived in 1500, and Portuguese colonization began after the Treaty of Tordesillas in 1494, which divided the New World between Spain and Portugal. Portuguese culture and language became dominant, alongside indigenous influences, shaping modern Brazilian identity.

Brazil's royal history began in 1808 when Prince Regent Dom João VI fled Napoleon and moved the Portuguese court to Brazil, elevating the country to the United Kingdom of Portugal, Brazil, and the Algarves. In 1822, Dom João's son, Dom Pedro I, declared Brazil's independence and became its first emperor. After his abdication in 1831, Dom Pedro II ruled until 1889, overseeing a period of economic growth, modernization, and the abolition of slavery.

In 1889, a military coup ended the monarchy, and Brazil became a republic. Today, the Brazilian royal family, the House of Orléans-Braganza, is led by Prince Bertrand, a descendant of Pedro II. Although there is no realistic possibility of restoring the monarchy, the family continues to promote Brazil's imperial history. The Imperial Palace in Rio de Janeiro, the family's former residence, remains a symbol of Brazil's imperial past.

---

2   https://www.britannica.com/place/Brazil/History

The People of Brazil

The people of Brazil are known for their rich cultural diversity, shaped by a mix of indigenous, African, European, and Asian influences. Brazil's population is predominantly of mixed descent, with a significant portion identifying as Pardo (multiracial), followed by White, Black, Asian, and Indigenous groups.

The country's large urban centers, particularly in the Southeast, such as São Paulo and Rio de Janeiro, are home to a bustling, cosmopolitan population, while rural areas, particularly in the North and Northeast, maintain strong connections to traditional lifestyles. Brazilians are famous for their warmth, hospitality, and strong sense of community, with family and social bonds playing a central role in daily life. Brazilian culture is also deeply intertwined with music, dance, and football (soccer), which serve as national unifiers. Despite facing social and economic disparities, Brazilians are known for their resilience and joy in celebrating life, as seen in their vibrant festivals like *Carnival* and *Festa Junina*.

Language

The official language of Brazil is Portuguese, making it the largest Portuguese-speaking country in the world. This linguistic heritage dates back to the 16th century when Portuguese explorers colonized Brazil. Over time, Brazilian Portuguese evolved with distinct regional accents, vocabulary, and expressions, influenced by indigenous languages, African languages brought by enslaved people, and immigrant languages such as Italian and German. While Portuguese is universally spoken, many indigenous languages are still used in native communities across the country. Brazilian Portuguese is known for its melodic tone and unique grammatical structures, and it plays a central role in shaping the country's identity and culture.

Religion

The major religion in Brazil is Roman Catholic, with a 49 percent majority. In fact, Brazil has the largest Catholic population in the world. The Catholic religion has a profound influence on Brazilian culture, society, and traditions. Catholic influence in Brazil is visible in the following so-cial-cultural aspects of daily life:

- **Cultural Practices:** Catholicism shapes many cultural practices and festivities in Brazil, such as Carnival, which incorporates religious themes and celebrations.

- **Social Values:** The Catholic Church promotes values such as family, community, and charity, which are integral to Brazilian society.

- **Education and Welfare:** The Church is involved in education and social services, operating numerous schools, hospitals, and charita-ble organizations across the country.

- **Political Influence:** The Catholic Church has historically played a role in Brazilian politics, advocating for social justice, human rights, and ethical governance.

Overall, Catholicism remains a significant component of Brazil's identity, impacting various aspects of daily life and national culture. Visiting the *Catedral Metropolitana Nossa Senhora Aparecida* (National Cathedral in Brasilia) is a great way to immerse yourself in the Catholic identity and culture that thrives throughout Brazil.

Brazil's Constitution guarantees the freedom of religion and other Evangelical Christian religions are also common in Brazil. Additionally, about two percent of the Brazilian population identifies with Afro-Brazilian religions such as *Candomblé* and *Umbanda*.

Affordability[3]

Brazil is generally more affordable than many other countries in the Western Hemisphere, with regions outside of major cities being even more budget friendly. The cost of living in Brazil is about half the cost in the United States, with rent about 400 percent less than in the United States. Despite Brazil's affordability, 24 percent of Brazil's population

---

3   https://wise.com/us/blog/cost-of-living-in-brazil#:~:text=Single%20
    person%20cost%20of%20living%20without%20rent&text=We'll%20
    dig%20into%20the,the%20US%20than%20in%20Brazil.

lives in poverty. The average net salary in Brazil is around R$2,347.90 per month (about US$400).

Groceries in Brazil are generally affordable, especially for tourists buying items with US dollars. However, many Brazilians face difficulties in accessing basic services, such as reliable energy supply for homes and essential cooking items for household use. For a single person, the cost of living in the United States is on average US$1,127 per month; in contrast, the cost of living in Brazil for a single person is on average US$571 per month. Then, for a family of four, the cost of living in the United States is on average US$4,109 per month; in contrast, the cost of living in Brazil is on average US$2,025 per month.

Financially, Brazil is one of the most unequal countries in the world, with 24 percent of the population living in extreme poverty. The income gap between the rich and the poor is among the highest in the world, contributing to widespread inequality.

Brazil, the Basics

How to Get There?

The easiest way to get to Brazil depends on your location, but generally, flying is the most convenient option. Major international airports in Brazil, such as São Paulo (**Guarulhos International Airport**), Rio de Janeiro (**Galeão International Airport**), and **Brasília International Airport**, are well-connected to destinations around the world. Most international flights to Brazil are direct, though some may require a layover, especially if you're traveling from smaller or less direct routes. Flights from the U.S. or Europe to Brazil typically take between 8-12 hours, depending on your departure city. For example, a direct flight from New York to Rio de Janeiro usually takes about 10 hours, while flying from London to São Paulo takes about 11-12 hours.

The cheapest times to fly to Brazil are during the low season from May to September, when demand is lower and fares are more affordable. The shoulder months of March and October also offer good deals, as they are just before or after peak travel periods. Avoid traveling during major holidays like Carnival (February/March) or New Year (December), as prices will be higher. Booking 3–6 months in advance, using fare comparison tools, and being flexible with your travel dates can help you find the best deals.

When to Visit?

The best time to visit Brazil is from April to June and September to November when the weather is mild, and there are fewer crowds and lower prices. If you're looking for a beach vacation or to experience Carnival (usually in February), the summer months from December to March are ideal, though it can be crowded and more expensive. For visiting the Amazon or Pantanal, the dry season (May to September) is the best time to go.

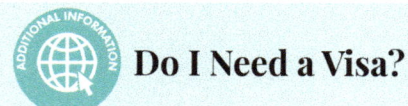 **Do I Need a Visa?**

Whether you need a visa for Brazil depends on your nationality and the purpose of your trip. Citizens of many countries, including the U.S., Canada, and EU nations, do not need a visa for tourism stays up to 90 days. However, you may need a visa for business, study, or longer stays. It's always best to check with the nearest Brazilian consulate or the Ministry of Foreign Affairs for the latest visa requirements.

How to Get Around

Brazil has modern and efficient public transportation, especially in major cities like São Paulo, Rio de Janeiro, Brasília, and Salvador. The most common mode of transport is buses, with fares ranging from R$4.40 (US$0.73) for local buses to US$10-30 for long-distance "executivo" buses. Metro systems are widely used in cities like São Paulo (the busiest metro system in the world), with single-ride fares averaging R$5.80 (US$0.96). Light rail trams also operate in several cities, with similar fares to the metro. Taxis are available 24/7 in major cities, with fares starting around R$5.40 (US$0.89). Digital travel passes can be used for buses, metros, and trams, while taxis can be flagged or booked via apps like Uber, 99Taxis, and Easy Taxi. Taxis are a safe and affordable option, especially when booked through a taxi stand or app.

Since Brazil is a huge country, flying is convenient way to brave longer routes. Brazil has almost 500 public airports, with three major international hubs: São Paulo Guarulhos International Airport, the busiest, handling over 26 million passengers annually; Rio de Janeiro Galeão Airport, serving 17 million passengers with two terminals offering shopping and services; and Brasília International Airport, serving 10 million passengers, focusing on domestic and some international flights. These airports are key entry points for travelers to Brazil's cities and regions.

 ## Monetary Advice

Brazil's official currency is the Brazilian Real (BRL), symbolized as R$. As of the latest data in 2024, the exchange rate fluctuates, but approximately:

- US$1 ~ R$5.00 to R$5.50
- €1 EUR ~ R$5.40 to R$6.00

Exchange rates can vary, so it's always a good idea to check the current rate before making any currency exchanges.

Credit and debit cards are also widely accepted in most urban areas, especially in restaurants, hotels, shopping malls, and larger tourist destinations. Major card networks like Visa, MasterCard, and American Express are commonly used. However, in more remote areas or smaller businesses, cash may still be preferred, and it's a good idea to have some local currency (Brazilian Real - BRL) on hand.

As for other currencies, Brazil primarily uses the Brazilian Real (BRL), and foreign currencies like USD, EUR, or others are generally not accepted for transactions. To use foreign currency, you'll need to exchange it for reais (plural for real) at a currency exchange office, bank, or ATM. ATMs are widely available in cities, and many allow you to withdraw Brazilian Real directly with your international debit or credit card, though they may charge fees for foreign transactions. Currency exchange kiosks at airports and major cities also provide services for converting foreign money into reais.

Bargaining and Tipping

Bargaining is generally not acceptable in formal stores, restaurants, or large retail chains in Brazil. However, it's common in street markets, local shops, and with street vendors, especially in tourist areas.

Tipping is not mandatory but appreciated. In restaurants, a service charge of around 10% is often included in the bill, but if it's not, leaving a tip of 10% is customary. For other services, like hotel staff or taxi drivers, rounding up the bill or leaving small tips is common, though not expected. In general, tipping is optional, but it is a nice way to show appreciation for good service.

Capital of Brazil, Brasilia[4]

In 1960, Brazil moved its capital from Rio de Janeiro to Brasília to promote national unity, economic development, and ease overcrowding in Rio. Designed with modern, symmetrical architecture resembling a bird in flight, Brasília serves as the hub for the Executive, Legislative, and Judiciary branches of government.

---

4   https://whc.unesco.org/en/list/445/#:~:text=Brasilia%2C%20a%20capital%20created%20ex,particular%2C%20are%20innovative%20and%20imaginative.

Located in the Brazilian highlands, the city features landmarks like the artificial Lake Paranoá and the Presidential Palace, Palacio da Alvorada. Brasília has a unique political structure, with no municipal government, unlike other federal cities like Washington, D.C. Although a young city, it ranks as Brazil's fourth-most populous. While Brasília reflects modern Brazilian history, it lacks colonial history, which can be explored in cities like Rio de Janeiro and Salvador. Key attractions include the National Congress, Cathedral of Brasília, Palácio da Alvorada, and the Botanical Garden of Brasília.

Brazil's Hospitality[5]

Brazilian hospitality is famously warm, friendly, and welcoming. Brazilians take great pride in making visitors feel at home, often going out of their way to offer help or share a meal. It's common for hosts to greet guests with hugs or cheek kisses (*beijos*), and small gifts or coffee (*cafezinho*) are frequently offered to visitors. Conversations are often lively, and small talk about football (soccer), music, or family is encouraged. Brazilians are known for their generosity and hospitality extends to making guests feel like part of the family, whether at a social gathering or in a more formal setting. Overall, the culture values warmth and personal connections, making it easy for travelers to feel welcomed and appreciated.

In Brazilian culture, politeness is centered around warmth, friendliness, and respect for social norms. Here are some tips on what is considered polite and impolite:

Polite Behaviors

1. **Arriving slightly late:** It's normal and even expected to arrive a few minutes late for social events. Being exactly on time may be seen as too formal or rigid.

---

5   https://www.connectbrazil.com/experience-brazils-hospitality/

2. **Greeting everyone:** Always greet everyone at a social gathering with a smile and a friendly *"Olá"* or other greetings, including cheek kisses or hugs in more informal settings.

3. **Light physical contact:** Brazilians are comfortable with light touches, like touching arms or shoulders during conversation, as it helps foster a personal connection.

4. **Accepting compliments:** Accept compliments graciously without downplaying them. Acknowledge them with appreciation.

5. **Small talk:** Engage in casual conversation, particularly about topics like football (soccer), music, or family, before moving to business matters or deeper discussions.

Impolite Behaviors

1. **Arriving exactly on time:** Punctuality is more relaxed for social events. Arriving too early or exactly on time can seem impolite or overly formal.

2. **Discussing sensitive topics:** Avoid talking about politics, business, or controversial subjects at social events, as this can make people uncomfortable.

3. **Blowing your nose or coughing in public:** These actions are seen as rude or inconsiderate, especially in social settings.

4. **Invading personal space:** While light touch is common, standing too close without it can be uncomfortable. Respect people's personal space, especially in more formal settings.

5. **Refusing hospitality:** If you're offered food, drinks, or a favor, it's polite to accept at least a small portion or thank the host for the offer, even if you don't want it.

CHAPTER 2

CUSTOMS

CHAPTER 2

CUSTOMS

Travelers Entering Brazil[6]

When traveling to Brazil, it is important to understand customs laws, including entry requirements and what items you can and cannot bring into the country. Being aware of this information before arriving at the airport can help you save both time and money.

To enter Brazil, your passport must be valid for at least **six months** before it expires. If your passport is valid but will expire in less than six months, Brazilian authorities will not allow you to enter the country. The reason for this requirement is that in the event of a medical emergency or an arrest, your travel plans could change unexpectedly. Brazil enforces this rule to ensure that you have the necessary documentation to return to your home country.

 Beginning April 10, 2025, travelers from most countries, including the United States, will require a visa. You can obtain an e-Visa by filling out an electronic application at **https://brazil.vfsevisa.com.**

---

6   https://br.usembassy.gov/u-s-citizen-services/#:~:text=You%20will%20
need:,all%20other%20types%20of%20travel

You may need to demonstrate sufficient financial means to fund your entire stay in Brazil as a tourist. Thus, you should print out copies of bank statements and credit card statements, showing your available balances and credit limit. Specifically, Brazil will require that tourists show that they have at least US$2,000 in funds to cover their expenses and any emergencies while traveling in Brazil.

You can expect the customs officer to inspect your passport at the immigrations and customs office at the airport. The officer will check to determine that your passport is sufficiently valid and that you have a valid visa before entering the country. You will have to show proof of funds during your e-visa application, and you should be ready to present copies of bank statements to the customs officer at the airport, if the officer requests updated evidence.

The maximum stay in Brazil for tourists is 90 days. However, the actual duration of your stay may be longer or shorter than 90 days, depending on your specific circumstances and the discretion of the customs official at the airport.

Visa Types[7]

Brazil grants several types of visas depending on the purpose of the visit and the duration of stay:

- **Tourist Visa (VIVIS):** This visa is for travelers visiting Brazil for tourism, leisure, or to attend cultural events. It typically allows for stays of up to 90 days.

- **Business Visa (VITEM II):** Issued to individuals traveling for business purposes, such as attending meetings, conferences, or exploring business opportunities. It is typically issued for up to 90 days within a 180-day period, but the specific duration can vary based on the purpose and nature of the business activities. In some cases, you can apply for an extension of your business visa, but it cannot

---

7   https://www.passportvisasexpress.com/visa_services/brazil/
country_news/brazilian_visa_types

exceed 180 days within a year. After that period, you may need to leave Brazil and reapply for a new visa.

- **Student Visa (VITEM IV):** Granted to individuals who have been accepted into educational institutions in Brazil for study purposes, from short courses to full-degree programs. It is typically valid for the duration of your academic program, usually ranging from 6 months to 1 year. It can be renewed if your studies continue, but the visa must be renewed annually while you're enrolled in a Brazilian educational institution.

- **Work Visa (VITEM V):** For foreigners who have secured employment in Brazil. This visa often requires a job offer from a Brazilian company and approval from the Ministry of Labor. Usually, it is valid for 1 to 2 years but can be renewed if the employment contract continues.

- **Temporary Visa (VITEM XIII):** This category includes several subcategories, such as visas for cultural exchanges, research, or missionary work. The initial validity is typically between 6 months to 2 years, depending on the specific category. Temporary visas can be extended, often for the same duration as the initial visa.

- **Permanent Visa:** Issued to individuals planning to reside permanently in Brazil, often applicable to family reunification cases, retirees, or those with substantial investments in the country.

- **Family Reunion:** For foreigners with family ties in Brazil who wish to settle and live in the country. Usually granted for 1 to 2 years initially, with the possibility of extension. After a few years of permanent residence, the individual may be eligible for permanent status in Brazil.

- **Diplomatic visa:** For diplomatic visitors that will enter Brazil for government purposes. Typically valid for the duration of the diplomatic mission (usually 1 to 5 years), depending on the specific purpose and appointment.

- **Official visa:** For government officials who will enter Brazil to conduct business on behalf of their government. Generally issued for the duration of the official government mission, which can range from a few days to a year or more, depending on the assignment.

- **Technical support visa:** For visitors who will provide technical support purposes, including resolving issues with products or services in a private company or government agency in Brazil. Typically granted for a period of up to 1 year, with the possibility of extension depending on the need for the technical support services.

- **Cruise visa:** For visitors who will enter Brazil as part of a cruise and intend to stay in the country for a short period until their vessel leaves the Brazilian port to its next location in the voyage. Typically granted for a period of up to 1 year, with the possibility of extension depending on the need for the technical support services.

- **Transit visa:** For visitors to Brazil who will spend a few hours in Brazil for transit purposes, until their flight or ship leaves for the next port of call. These visas are mostly utilized for travelers with a layover flight in a Brazilian airport. Usually valid for a short period, typically up to 72 hours, allowing the traveler to transit through Brazil to their next destination.

Each visa type has its own requirements and application procedures, which generally involve submitting necessary documentation and attending an interview at a Brazilian consulate or embassy.

Entry Entitlements

Brazilian immigration and customs authorities have strict guidelines on what can and cannot be brought into the country, including restrictions on duty-free items and currency. Travelers must adhere to these regulations to ensure a smooth entry.

Personal items for personal use, such as clothing and electronics, are generally exempt from customs duties, but excessive quantities may raise concerns. Duty-free allowances include up to 12 liters of alcohol, 10 packs of cigarettes, and goods worth up to US$500 (or US$1,000 for air or sea passengers). Prohibited items include illegal drugs, weapons, certain plants, endangered species products, and counterfeit goods. Certain food products, especially fresh meat and dairy, are restricted, and over-the-counter medications are allowed in reasonable amounts.

Travelers must declare currency exceeding R$10,000 (US$1,649), and pets require specific health documentation.

When entering Brazil, it's essential to declare anything you bring that exceeds the allowed limits (such as alcohol, tobacco, or electronics). Failing to do so may result in fines or confiscation of items. You can check the Brazilian Customs website or consult with your airline before traveling for the most up-to-date information on entry requirements and customs regulations.

Monetary Instruments and Restrictions[8]

One of the primary restrictions pertains to the declaration of currency amounts. Visitors to Brazil can bring any amount of foreign currency into the country; however, amounts exceeding R$10,000 (approximately US$2,000) must be declared upon entry. This declaration is crucial, as failing to report amounts above this limit can result in confiscation or fines. Furthermore, travelers carrying undeclared cash exceeding this threshold may face legal consequences and complications with law enforcement. Any amount below the threshold does not require declaration, which streamlines the entry process for tourists.

In addition to cash, travelers must also be aware of restrictions involving other monetary instruments like traveler's checks, credit cards, and debit cards. Transactions up to US$3,000 require only an official identification document for processing, while larger transactions may necessitate additional documentation.[9] This includes proof of source or ownership of the funds, especially when traveling with significant sums or engaging in foreign currency transactions. It is advisable for travelers to carry necessary documents to facilitate smooth financial transactions, particularly if planning to utilize large amounts.

---

8   https://www.gov.br/mre/pt-br/consulado-londres/useful-information/visiting-brazil#:~:text=please%20click%20here.-,Bringing%20money%20into%20Brazil,when%20arriving%20in%20Brazil%22%20page

9   https://www.bcb.gov.br/en/financialstability/fxtravelbrazil

 Non-compliance with Brazilian currency regulations can lead to significant hassles for travelers. Besides the potential confiscation of undeclared funds, travelers may encounter lengthy legal processes and fines. Therefore, it is imperative to remain informed about and adhere to these regulations, ensuring a seamless travel experience while exploring the vibrant culture and landscapes of Brazil.

 Restricted and Prohibited Items

When traveling to Brazil, there are specific restricted and prohibited items you should be aware of to avoid any issues at customs. These items are regulated to protect public health, safety, and the environment.

Prohibited Items:

1. **Illegal Drugs and Narcotics**: All forms of illegal drugs, including marijuana, cocaine, and other controlled substances, are strictly banned.

2. **Weapons and Ammunition**: Firearms, ammunition, explosives, and other weaponry are prohibited unless you have special authorization from Brazilian authorities.

3. **Endangered Species Products**: The import of products made from endangered species (e.g., ivory, tortoiseshell, furs) is prohibited by international wildlife protection agreements.

4. **Counterfeit Goods**: Fake or pirated items, such as counterfeit designer clothing, electronics, and accessories, are banned.

5. **Unregulated Pharmaceuticals**: Certain drugs and medicines that are not approved by Brazilian health authorities are not allowed, especially those containing narcotics or psychotropic substances.

6. **Pornographic Materials:** Obscene or pornographic materials are prohibited for import into Brazil.

Restricted Items:

1. *Food Products:*

   ▪ **Meats, Dairy, and Other Perishables:** These items are highly regulated, and some may be restricted or require special permits. Bring only packaged, non-perishable food for personal use.

   ▪ **Fresh Fruits and Vegetables:** Most fresh produce is not allowed due to the risk of pests and disease.

2. *Plants and Seeds:*

   ▪ **Live Plants, Seeds, and Soil:** Brazil has strict regulations to prevent the spread of pests and diseases. Bringing plants or seeds without the proper certification or permits is prohibited.

3. *Medicines:*

   ▪ **Prescription Drugs:** While personal medications are allowed, they must be in their original packaging and accompanied by a doctor's prescription. Some medications containing controlled substances may require additional documentation.

   ▪ **Unapproved Medications:** Certain over-the-counter medications that are legal in other countries may be restricted in Brazil. Always check the specific regulations before traveling with medications.

4. *Alcohol and Tobacco:*

   ▪ Travelers are allowed to bring up to 12 liters of alcohol and 10 packs of cigarettes or equivalent tobacco products duty-free. However, bringing excessive amounts could result in extra scrutiny.

5. Currency:

- If carrying more than R$10,000 (U.S. Dollar $1,649) (or the equivalent in other currencies), travelers must declare it upon arrival. This applies to cash, traveler's checks, or banknotes.

Travelers may also be subject to arrest if the prohibited item is considered dangerous and a threat to the public health and safety. You can be subject to both criminal and civil penalties for bringing prohibited items into Brazil. If you're uncertain if a specific item is allowed into Brazil, it's advisable not to bring it with you on your trip. You may also contact the Brazilian consulate to obtain clarification on what goods are prohibited.

Five Practical Tips to Know Before You Go

1. **Greeting Customs:** Brazilians greet each other warmly with hugs or kisses on the cheek (one in São Paulo, two in Rio). Be ready to reciprocate these friendly gestures to make a good first impression.

2. **Time Perceptions:** Brazilians often run on "Brazilian time," meaning social events can start later than scheduled. Be patient and embrace the laid-back pace.

3. **Cuisine Etiquette:** Lunch is the main meal, typically served between 12 PM and 2 PM, while dinner is lighter and later. If invited to someone's home, try everything offered and show gratitude.

4. **Soccer Culture:** Football (soccer) is a huge part of Brazilian culture. Engaging in conversations about local teams like Flamengo or São Paulo FC will help you connect with locals, especially during major soccer matches.

5. **Communication Styles:** Brazilians are expressive, using hand gestures and maintaining eye contact. Avoid public confrontation or criticism, and express disagreements tactfully to keep things harmonious.

CRIME IN BRAZIL

CRIME IN BRAZIL

Overview[10]

Understanding crime statistics and information is essential for making informed decisions while traveling, yet travelers should not allow this data to induce fear. Brazil faces high crime rates, especially in major cities like Rio de Janeiro and São Paulo, and the threat of street crime is expanding into rural areas. Tourists are often targets of pickpocketing and theft, which can occur at any time, particularly in crowded places and especially at night. Even in affluent neighborhoods, no area is completely safe, making it crucial for travelers to exercise caution by securing passports and important documents in hotel safes and carrying only copies in public.

Common crime scenarios involve pickpocketing at airports, hotel lobbies, markets, and on public transportation. Tourists should avoid displaying valuables or falling victim to scams disguised as offers of help. Monitoring financial accounts for unauthorized ATM or credit card transactions is advisable, as fraudulent charges may appear post-travel. Crime rates tend to spike near beaches, nightlife, and tourist spots, particularly during events like Carnival. Although many Brazilian cities have established tourist police to enhance security, tourists must remain vigilant and informed about local conditions.

---

10   https://www.statista.com/topics/7017/crime-and-violence-in-brazil/

In the political context, following the closely contested 2022 presidential election, Brazil has seen significant civil unrest and riots, particularly among supporters of Luiz Inácio Lula da Silva and Jair Bolsonaro. This political polarization has led to increased violence and challenges for the new government as it seeks to mitigate unrest and stabilize the nation. The interplay between political unrest and crime highlights the importance of staying aware of local advisories and having emergency contacts readily available, while also avoiding large gatherings when necessary.

Crime Hotspots in Brazil

Brazil, known for its vibrant culture and stunning landscapes, unfortunately, also grapples with significant crime challenges, particularly in certain areas designated as crime hotspots. Understanding these locations can help both locals and visitors navigate safely and avoid potential dangers.

Brasília faces significant crime, especially in affluent neighborhoods, tourist areas, and at the Central Bus Station, where drug-related activities are common. Crime rates have risen in recent years, with incidents happening randomly. In Rio de Janeiro, tourists are at risk of street thefts, robberies, and violent attacks, particularly near major attractions and during Carnival. Sao Paulo also experiences high rates of armed robbery, particularly at stoplights, in red-light districts, and upscale restaurants, with criminals targeting electronics, luxury items, and using drugs to incapacitate victims.

Crime Statistics[11]

Brazil has long struggled with high crime rates, marked particularly by violent crimes such as homicides, thefts, and drug-related incidents. According to recent statistics, the homicide rate in Brazil was approximately 21.3 per 100,000 inhabitants in 2021, reflecting a consistent

---

11   https://www.statista.com/topics/7017/crime-and-violence-in-brazil/

concern regarding violence in both urban and rural areas.[12] Notably, cities like Rio de Janeiro and São Paulo are often featured prominently in discussions of crime statistics due to their high rates of gang-related violence and street crime.

The Brazilian Public Security Forum reports that issues of socio-economic inequality and inadequate law enforcement resources contribute to the prevalence of crime across the country. For instance, regions with significant poverty often see elevated crime rates as communities face challenges such as unemployment and lack of social services. Furthermore, recent efforts to improve public safety, including increased police presence and community outreach programs, have shown some promise in addressing crime trends, but challenges remain pervasive, particularly in areas heavily impacted by drug trafficking and organized crime. Understanding crime statistics in Brazil is vital for both residents and visitors, as it aids in making informed decisions about safety and security while navigating the country.

To illustrate the trend, here are some recent numbers related to crime in Brazil:

- **Homicide rates:** Brazil's homicide rate was 22.8 per 100,000 Brazilians in 2023, the lowest since 2012. In 2022, Brazil recorded 46,000 murders, and most victims were men.
- **Robbery resulting in death:** There were 953 such incidents in Brazil in 2023, which constitutes a 23.64 percent drop percent from 2022.
- **Corruption:** In 2023, the Brazilian Federal police increased its corruption investigations, resulting in 147 arrests, 2091 search and seizure warrants, and R$897 million in illicit goods and valuables seized.
- **Rape and statutory rape:** Rape remains significant concern in Brazil, with cases continuing to rise despite underreporting.

---

12 https://www.unodc.org/documents/data-and-analysis/gsh/2023/GSH23_ExSum.pdf

Quick Safety Tips

- **Be aware of your surroundings:** Be aware of what's happening around you and keep your belongings close.

- **Avoid certain areas:** Avoid protests, large public gatherings, and areas where illicit activities occur. In popular spring break destinations, exercise extra caution in downtown areas, especially after dark.

- **Be careful with your belongings:** Don't draw attention to your money or business affairs. Keep a photocopy of your passport and other important documents separate from the originals. Store valuables in a safe place.

- **Be careful with alcohol:** Be mindful of your alcohol intake and be aware of counterfeit alcohol.

- **Stay connected:** Keep your phone charged and share your travel plans with friends or family.

- **Know who to call:** Make a list of emergency phone numbers and keep them handy.

- **Check the travel advisory:** Check your government's travel advisory for the most up-to-date information.

- **Bring extra cash:** It's not unusual for a doctor or hospital to demand payment in cash for emergency medical attention.

CRIMINAL LAW VIOLATIONS

IN THIS CHAPTER

- Marijuana in Brazil
- Law of The Land Hypothetical
- Other Drugs in Brazil
- Law of The Land Hypothetical
- Prescription Medications
- Takeaways

CRIMINAL LAW VIOLATIONS

Marijuana in Brazil[13]

Marijuana legalization in Brazil has evolved over time, with strict prohibitionist policies gradually shifting. In 2006, Brazil decriminalized small-scale drug possession, replacing jail time with alternative penalties like community service. The conversation around medical marijuana began in the 2010s, with Brazil allowing the import of cannabidiol (CBD) in 2015 for medical use, especially for epilepsy. By 2019, cannabis-based products were permitted in pharmacies with a prescription, though recreational marijuana remains illegal. While penalties for personal possession are now less severe, trafficking remains a serious crime with prison sentences. The legal treatment of marijuana continues to be a contentious issue, especially regarding its enforcement and social implications.

 **Law of the Land Hypothetical**

HYPOTHETICAL: *Raul is traveling through Brazil when he is stopped by the police. Upon searching his bag, the officers find a small amount of*

---

13   https://www.researchgate.net/
    publication/262741177_The_history_of_marihuana_in_Brazil

cannabis that contains more than 0.2% THC. Raul informs the po-
lice that he has a medical marijuana card for a terminal illness and
that the cannabis is for personal use, in accordance with his doctor's
prescription.

Given the legal context of cannabis in Brazil, should the police allow
Raul to proceed without further action?

ANSWER: *Yes, the police should allow Raul to proceed without further*
incident. According to Brazilian law, while cannabis remains illegal for
recreational use, it has been decriminalized for personal use in small
quantities. Specifically, the Supreme Court has ruled that individu-
als can possess up to 40 grams of cannabis for personal consumption,
and those with terminal illnesses are legally permitted to use canna-
bis-based medications. Raul's medical card and confirmation that the
cannabis is for personal use should exempt him from legal penalties.
However, it's important to note that cannabis commercialization (e.g.,
selling or trafficking) remains illegal in Brazil. Therefore, Raul is not
in violation of any laws as long as the cannabis is for personal medical
use.

Other Drugs in Brazil[14]

In Brazil, the penalties for possessing drugs other than marijuana differ
significantly based on the classification of the substance involved. The
legal framework established by Law 11.343 in 2006, categorizes drugs
into two main groups: 1) those intended for personal use, and 2) those
related to trafficking.

Possession of controlled substances like cocaine, crack cocaine, and heroin is treated more severely than marijuana. Individuals caught with these
illicit drugs face criminal charges that can lead to significantly harsher
penalties, which may include imprisonment. For example, possession
of these substances generally results in a range of penalties, which can

---

14   https://www.loc.gov/law/help/decriminalization-of-narcotics/
     brazil.php#:~:text=Brazil%20has%20not%20decriminalized%20
     narcotics,drugs%20for%20alleged%20personal%20use

extend from six months to five years of imprisonment. However, judges may consider various factors, including the amount of the substance and the individual's intent, which can lead to alternative penalties such as rehabilitation programs instead of incarceration, particularly for first-time offenders.

Moreover, Brazil's approach to drug policy often emphasizes a punitive stance on trafficking, with severe consequences, including extensive prison sentences—ranging from five to fifteen years—focused on deterring drug-related crime. The vagueness in distinguishing between personal use and trafficking can lead to inconsistencies in law enforcement, disproportionately affecting marginalized populations who may be caught with less significant amounts.

 **Law of the Land Hypothetical**

HYPOTHETICAL: *Raul is stopped by the police while walking through a busy street in Brazil. The officers search his bag and discover a large quantity of cannabis, along with other illegal substances. Raul does not have a medical card to justify the possession of the cannabis, and he cannot provide any legal explanation for the large amounts of drugs in his possession. What are the potential consequences Raul may face, and will the police arrest him?*

ANSWER: *Raul is likely to be arrested due to the large quantity of cannabis and other illegal substances, as possession without valid justification is illegal in Brazil. However, police discretion may allow him to be released with a warning, especially if he cooperates or is a first-time offender. If arrested, a judge will assess Raul's intent and whether the substances were for personal use or trafficking. Trafficking would lead to harsher penalties, including imprisonment, while personal use could result in a more lenient, rehabilitative approach.*

Prescription Medication

When traveling to Brazil, travelers are indeed allowed to bring prescription medication for personal use; however, specific regulations must be followed to ensure compliance with Brazilian laws. It is crucial that individuals carry their medications in their original containers, clearly labeled with the prescription details, including the traveler's name and the prescribing doctor's information. This is particularly important for controlled substances, which may be subject to stricter scrutiny upon arrival.[15]

Additionally, travelers are advised to bring along a copy of the prescription, as well as any necessary documentation, such as a doctor's letter that outlines the need for the medication, especially if it includes drugs that are regulated in Brazil. The quantity of medication should be reasonable and consistent with the duration and purpose of treatment, ensuring it does not appear that one is attempting to import medications for commercial purposes.

Brazil's National Health Surveillance Agency (*ANVISA*) recommends that individuals check their specific medications against existing regulations before traveling. Some medications may be prohibited or require special authorization, so consulting ANVISA's guidelines or the nearest Brazilian consulate is advisable for the most accurate and updated information. By adhering to these regulations, travelers can facilitate a smoother entry process and ensure their medications are permitted.

 **Takeaways**

- Possession of small amounts (up to 40g or six plants) of cannabis for personal use is decriminalized, with penalties like community service, not incarceration.

---

15   https://www.gov.br/mre/pt-br/consulado-londres/useful-information/visiting-brazil

- Medical use of cannabis, particularly CBD, is legal with a prescription, but cannabis commercialization remains illegal.

- Trafficking marijuana carries 5-15 years in prison, while possession for personal use results in alternative penalties. Enforcement can vary based on socio-economic factors.

- Possessing large quantities of marijuana without a valid reason (e.g., medical card) can lead to arrest, with the court determining if it's for personal use or trafficking.

- Possession of drugs like cocaine and heroin is severely penalized, with harsh sentences for trafficking.

- Travelers can bring prescription medications but must carry them in original containers with a prescription. Controlled substances may require special authorization from ANVISA.

ALCOHOL-RELATED OFFENSES

ALCOHOL-RELATED OFFENSES

Alcohol-Related Offenses

Alcohol, particularly cachaça and beer, plays a central role in Brazilian culture and social life. *Cachaça*, Brazil's national liquor, has historical roots dating back to the colonial era, while beer is the most widely consumed alcoholic beverage today, especially during gatherings like Carnival and *churrascos* (barbecues). Alcohol is seen as a social activity, enjoyed in communal settings with friends and family. While alcohol remains an important part of celebrations and festivals, concerns over excessive drinking and its social consequences have grown in recent years, prompting public health initiatives. Despite these issues, alcohol continues to be deeply intertwined with Brazil's identity and cultural practices.

Brazil is known for a variety of iconic drinks, including the *Caipirinha*, a cocktail made with cachaça, lime, and sugar; cachaça itself, a sugarcane spirit central to Brazilian culture; and *Guaraná*, a popular soft drink made from an Amazonian fruit. Beer (*cerveja*) is widely consumed, especially lagers like Skol and Brahma, often enjoyed at social gatherings. *Batida*, a fruit-flavored cocktail with cachaça, and *Açaí* smoothies, popular in coastal areas, are also common. Additionally, Mate (*chimarrão*), a traditional herbal tea, is especially popular in southern Brazil. These drinks reflect Brazil's rich cultural diversity and tropical flavors.

Alcohol is legal and widely available in Brazil. The legal drinking age is 18, and alcohol can be purchased at a variety of locations, including supermarkets, convenience stores, bars, restaurants, and nightclubs. Alcohol is commonly consumed at parties, beach gatherings, and festivals like Carnival, and it is served alongside popular local foods. There are also specific regulations regarding alcohol consumption in public places, especially in relation to safety and public disturbances, but generally, alcohol consumption is a significant part of daily life and Brazilian hospitality.

However, there are alcohol-free zones in certain cities or events (like near schools), and some municipalities have laws restricting the sale of alcohol during certain hours or on certain days, especially during holidays or election periods.

Alcohol Regulation

The penalties for alcohol-related violations are significantly enforced, particularly focusing on drunk driving and public intoxication. The *Brazilian Traffic Code* imposes strict consequences for driving under the influence, with a zero-tolerance policy established in 2008, meaning any measurable blood alcohol content (BAC) can lead to punitive action.[16] Individuals found driving with a BAC above this threshold face severe penalties, including fines that can reach up to R$2,934.70 (US$497.14), a mandatory suspension of their driver's license for a period of 12 months, vehicle impoundment, and possible jail time for repeat offenders. Moreover, for those charged with offenses leading to accidents or injuries while under the influence, the penalties can escalate dramatically, resulting in significant prison sentences ranging from two to ten years, depending on the severity of the incident.[17] In addition to traffic-related violations, public intoxication can lead to arrest and fines in certain municipalities, highlighting Brazil's commitment to maintaining public safety and order regarding alcohol consumption.

---

16   https://en.wikipedia.org/wiki/Drunk_driving_law_by_country

17   https://seriousaccidents.com/blog/
brazil-passes-one-of-the-toughest-dui-laws-in-the-world

 **Things to Remember**

- **Drinking Age:** The legal drinking age in Brazil is 18 years old.

- **ID:** To purchase alcohol or be served at bars and clubs, individuals may be asked for proof of age, typically in the form of an official ID such as a national ID card (for Brazilian citizens) or a passport (for foreign tourists).

- **Public Consumption:** Public alcohol consumption is generally allowed in Brazil, including at beaches, parks, and public events. However, local laws or municipal regulations may impose restrictions in certain areas (e.g., near schools, public transport stations, or certain tourist zones).

- **Public Intoxication:** Public intoxication is not illegal in Brazil, but disorderly conduct (e.g., causing disturbances, fighting, or damaging property while intoxicated) can lead to fines or arrest. In some cities, drinking in public places may be banned after certain hours, especially in heavily populated tourist areas.

- **Drunk Driving:** Brazil has a zero tolerance policy for drinking and driving. Any trace of alcohol in the blood is punishable by severe penalties, including heavy fines, imprisonment, and license suspension. The legal limit for alcohol in the blood is effectively zero for drivers, with authorities employing breathalyzer tests.

- **Purchase of Alcohol:** Alcohol can be purchased at supermarkets, convenience stores, bars, restaurants, and liquor stores. No specific permits are required for individuals to buy alcohol as long as they are above the legal drinking age (18 years old).

- **Alcohol Permits:** In general, individuals do not need special permits to buy or consume alcohol. However, bars, restaurants, and venues that serve alcohol may need a license from local authorities to legally operate, especially in regulated environments like tourist hotspots.

- **Illegal Alcohol:** The sale of illegal alcohol is prohibited, including counterfeit alcohol or alcohol without proper regulation and labeling. Importing or selling alcohol without meeting government regulations (e.g., customs duties, proper labeling) is also illegal. Alcohol sold on the black market or by unlicensed vendors is subject to legal penalties.

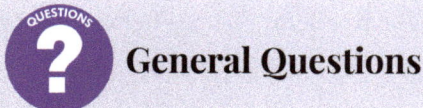 **General Questions**

1. *Is it illegal to drink alcohol in public places in Brazil?* No. Drinking alcohol in public places is generally allowed in Brazil, but local laws and regulations can vary. For example, some cities, especially in tourist areas or near schools and hospitals, may impose restrictions on alcohol consumption in public spaces. In many cases, authorities can issue fines or ask individuals to stop drinking if the public consumption is seen as a disturbance or violation of local ordinances.

2. *What are the penalties for driving under the influence of alcohol (DUI) in Brazil?* Brazil has strict laws regarding driving under the influence (DUI). The legal blood alcohol concentration (BAC) limit for drivers is 0.05%. However, drivers caught with a BAC higher than 0.34% face severe penalties, including a fine, suspension of their driver's license for 12 months, and possible detention. In cases of DUI resulting in accidents or injuries, penalties can be even more severe, including imprisonment. Enforcement is strict, and law enforcement authorities frequently conduct sobriety checkpoints.

3. ***Can individuals be arrested for public intoxication in Brazil?***
   Public intoxication in Brazil is generally not a criminal offense on
   its own. However, if a person is visibly intoxicated and engages
   in disruptive behavior—such as causing a public disturbance, en-
   dangering their own safety or the safety of others, or engaging in
   acts of aggression—they can be arrested for disturbing the peace
   or other related offenses. Brazilian law allows police officers to
   detain individuals who are behaving dangerously or violently
   while intoxicated, even if the mere state of drunkenness itself
   isn't a crime. This is more likely in cases where the individual's
   behavior negatively impacts public order.

Law of the Land Hypothetical

HYPOTHETICAL: *Raul is visiting Brazil and enjoying the vibrant nightlife. On a Sunday night, he purchases beer and wine from a convenience store with no restrictions, as alcohol is legally available for sale
late at night. Raul drinks alcohol while walking along the beach and
in public spaces without issue, but when he enters a soccer stadium to
watch a match, he continues drinking his beer.*

*Is Raul violating any laws, and how should the police respond if they
catch him drinking in the stadium?*

ANSWER: *Raul is indeed violating a specific rule by consuming alcohol
inside the soccer stadium, as drinking alcohol is prohibited in such
venues in Brazil. While Raul can legally purchase and consume alcohol in public spaces like streets and bars, soccer stadiums are an excep-
tion. Upon being caught by police, Raul would likely receive an initial
warning. However, if he continues to drink in the stadium despite the
warning, the authorities may impose harsher penalties, including fines
or other legal actions.*

*It's important to note that interactions with police officers in Brazil tend
to be more informal, and serious escalation usually happens only if
the individual responds aggressively or belligerently. Therefore, if Raul
remains polite and compliant, he can avoid more severe consequences.*

Additionally, Raul should be aware that while public alcohol consumption is generally allowed, local rules like the stadium ban must still be followed.

CHAPTER 6

FIREARM & AMMUNITION OFFENSES

IN THIS CHAPTER

- Current Firearm Status
- Firearm-Related Penalties
- Traveling with Firearms
- General Questions
- Law of the Land Hypothetical

FIREARM & AMMUNITION OFFENSES

Current Firearm Status[18]

The main law governing firearm ownership in Brazil is Law No. 10.826/2003, also known as the Disarmament Statute, which regulates the acquisition, registration, and use of firearms in the country. Under this law, Brazilian citizens can legally own firearms, but there are strict requirements and procedures to follow.

Key Requirements for Gun Ownership

- **Minimum Age:** The individual must be at least 25 years old.

- **No Criminal Record:** The applicant must not have a criminal record, nor any history of involvement in domestic violence or mental health issues.

- **Psychological Evaluation and Training:** Applicants must undergo psychological tests and firearm handling training at accredited institutions.

- **Justification of Need:** Applicants need to provide a justifiable reason for owning a firearm, such as personal defense, sports shooting, or hunting. This is one of the key hurdles for legal gun ownership.

---

18 https://www.aljazeera.com/news/2023/7/21/
brazil-to-rein-in-gun-ownership-after-bolsonaro-era-expansion

In recent years, under the government of President Jair Bolsonaro (2019-2023), Brazil saw a significant relaxation of certain restrictions, with executive decrees allowing easier access to firearms for civilians, especially for those living in rural areas, and for people engaged in activities like hunting and shooting sports. However, these decrees faced significant pushback from various sectors, including public safety advocates and lawmakers, who warned about increased violence and social instability.

Gun Carrying

Brazilian law does not allow the general population to carry firearms in public. Carrying firearms in public is tightly regulated and typically limited to police officers, military personnel, and other security professionals. However, individuals with special permits (such as those in certain professional sectors or individuals who can demonstrate a heightened risk of personal threat) may be allowed to carry firearms, though this is rare.

The Disarmament Statute does allow for the use of firearms in self-defense situations, but the use of force must be proportionate. This means that individuals who use firearms in defense must prove they acted in a manner necessary to protect themselves from imminent danger. Any excessive use of force could result in criminal liability.

Gun Violence and Crime

Brazil has historically had a high rate of gun violence, with firearms being involved in a significant percentage of homicides. In 2021, firearms were used in around 70 percent of homicides in the country, and Brazil has consistently ranked among the countries with the highest rates of firearm-related deaths.

Due to this, there has been an ongoing debate about the regulation of firearms, particularly concerning whether looser laws (allowing easier access to guns) increase or decrease violence. Proponents argue that law-abiding citizens should have the right to protect themselves, while opponents warn that more guns on the streets will lead to more violence.

Firearm Registration and Control

All firearms in Brazil must be registered with the Federal Police. The registration process involves a series of checks, including background investigations and verifying the need for the firearm. Gun owners must also renew their registration every five years and comply with safety standards. Failure to register a firearm can result in penalties, including imprisonment.

There is also a buyback program in place, through which individuals can voluntarily surrender firearms, helping to reduce the number of illegal weapons in circulation.

Current Legislative Outlook

While the Disarmament Statute remains the cornerstone of Brazil's firearm regulation, the country is currently grappling with conflicting pressures on gun ownership. Supporters of gun rights have called for further deregulation, arguing that law-abiding citizens should be able to carry arms for protection in a country where violence is rampant. On the other hand, public safety advocates and human rights groups argue that more access to guns will only exacerbate Brazil's gun violence problem. New President, Lula da Silva (2023 - present), has signaled intentions to tighten restrictions on gun ownership and control after the policies of the previous administration made it easier to own and carry firearms. Under Lula's government, there has been an effort to reverse some of the more permissive policies introduced during Bolsonaro's presidency, emphasizing stricter background checks, training, and monitoring.

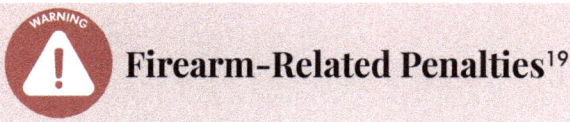

Firearm-Related Penalties[19]

In Brazil, firearm-related penalties are governed primarily by the Disarmament Statute (Law No. 10.826/2003), along with other criminal provisions in the Penal Code. The penalties for firearm offenses can be severe, and they vary depending on the nature of the violation:

- **Illegal Possession or Carrying:** Up to 4 years of imprisonment and fines if caught with an unregistered firearm, unless authorized.

- **Firearm Trafficking:** 3 to 6 years in prison and fines; harsher penalties if the firearm is used in another crime.

- **Modification of Firearms:** 3 to 6 years in prison and fines for altering firearms, such as changing serial numbers.

- **Use of Firearm in a Crime:** Additional prison time for using a firearm in crimes, such as murder or robbery, with sentences increased based on the offense.

- **Possession Without Justifiable Reason:** 2 to 4 years in prison if a firearm is owned without legitimate justification (self-defense, hunting, etc.).

- **Illegal Possession of Ammunition:** 1 to 3 years in prison, depending on the amount and type of ammunition.

- **Carrying Firearms in Restricted Areas:** 1 to 3 years in prison or fines for carrying firearms in places like airports or public buildings without authorization.

- **Carrying Under the Influence:** 1 to 3 years in prison for carrying a firearm while intoxicated by alcohol or drugs.

---

19 http://pretoria.itamaraty.gov.br/en-us/customs_regulations_in_brazil.
xml#:~:text=).%20Brazilians%20and%20foreigners%20entering%20
Brazil,the%20remainder%20of%20the%20traveler's

- **Failure to Surrender Firearm:** 1 to 3 years in prison if ordered to surrender a firearm (e.g., in domestic violence cases) and failure to comply.

- **Registration Violations:** Penalties, including fines or imprisonment, for failing to register or renew firearm ownership.

Traveling with Firearms

Traveling to Brazil with firearms is permitted but heavily regulated, necessitating adherence to specific legal requirements to ensure compliance with Brazilian law. Travelers intending to bring firearms or ammunition into the country must be registered with the Brazilian government and typically need to provide a variety of documentation, including an International Import Certificate (CII) issued by the Brazilian Armed Forces.[20] Furthermore, they must possess a valid firearm license in their home country, demonstrate a legitimate purpose for importing the weapon—such as sports shooting or hunting—and present all relevant documents upon entry. It is advisable for travelers to consult the Brazilian consulate or embassy prior to travel to confirm the latest updates.

Given Brazil's strict stance on gun control, individuals must approach international travel with firearms with caution and thorough preparation to avoid complications during their visit.[21]

---

20 https://thebrazilbusiness.com/article/
how-to-import-guns-and-ammunition-to-brazil

21 https://www.trade.gov/country-commercial-guides/
brazil-temporary-entry

? General Questions

1. *What are the penalties for possessing a firearm without proper authorization in Brazil?* In Brazil, possessing a firearm without proper authorization is a serious offense. The penalty for illegal possession or carrying of a firearm is typically 2 to 4 years of imprisonment, along with a fine. This applies to individuals who do not have the required registration or a valid permit to own or carry a firearm.

2. *Can a person legally carry a firearm in public in Brazil?* Generally, carrying firearms in public is prohibited in Brazil unless the individual has special authorization. Special permits may be granted to certain professionals, such as police officers, military personnel, or people facing specific threats. Without such a permit, carrying a firearm in public can lead to imprisonment of 2 to 4 years. Individuals may also face additional penalties if they carry firearms in restricted areas, such as near schools, airports, or government buildings.

3. *What are the consequences of using a firearm in the commission of a crime in Brazil?* Using a firearm during the commission of a crime significantly aggravates the penalty. For example, if a firearm is used in the commission of a homicide, the sentence for murder can increase substantially. The penalty for qualified homicide (when a firearm is used) can range from 12 to 30 years of imprisonment depending on the circumstances. In cases of armed robbery, assault, or other violent crimes, the presence of a firearm typically leads to harsher sentences, reflecting the gravity of the offense and the potential for harm caused by the weapon.

 **Law of the Land Hypothetical**

HYPOTHETICAL: *Raul, a licensed firearms owner, is planning a trip to Brazil and wishes to bring his Glock pistol for personal use during his stay. He wants to ensure that he follows all necessary legal procedures to avoid any issues with Brazilian authorities. What steps must Raul follow to legally bring a Glock firearm into Brazil for personal use?*

ANSWER: *If Raul is traveling to Brazil with a Glock, he must follow a series of legal steps to ensure the firearm is allowed entry:*

1. **Declare the Firearm with the Airline:** *Raul must declare the firearm to the airline and pack it securely in the baggage hold according to airline guidelines.*

2. **Present the Firearm to Brazilian Customs:** *Upon arrival in Brazil, Raul must present his firearm to Customs for inspection, where it will be temporarily retained.*

3. **Submit a Written Request to the Brazilian Army:** *Raul needs to submit a written request for firearm clearance from the Brazilian Army, including an international import certificate and an explanation for bringing the firearm into Brazil (e.g., for sport shooting or self-defense).*

4. **Army Review:** *The Brazilian Army will review Raul's request and, if satisfied, approve the importation of the firearm.*

5. **Customs Authority Decision:** *After Army approval, Customs will make the final decision. Only if Customs grants clearance will Raul be able to retrieve the firearm and proceed with his plans.*

PROSTITUTION

IN THIS CHAPTER

- Overview
- Legality and Penalties
- Prostitution Practices
- Sex Trafficking and Exploitation
- Sex Tourism and Public Implications
- Tips to Avoid Being Solicited
- General Questions
- Law of the Land Hypothetical

CHAPTER 7

PROSTITUTION

Overview[22]

Prostitution is **legal** in Brazil, as there are no laws prohibiting two con-
senting adults from exchanging money for sex. Professional sex workers can advertise and practice their trade without fear of police raids or
criminal penalties. Similarly, customers can engage in such exchanges
without concern for legal consequences. In contrast to other countries,
there are no municipal laws that restrict prostitution to certain zones in
the city.[23] Instead, Brazilians tend to have a nonchalant attitude toward
prostitution, and the practice does not carry the stigma that it does in
the United States.

However, there are two main exceptions in Brazil to the laxity for conduct that constitutes prostitution. First, establishing a brothel is considered pimping and as such, it is illegal. The owner of such an establishment may face the closure of the business as well as criminal penalties.
Second, pursuant to Articles 244-247 of the Brazilian Constitution and
the Penal Code, prostitution with a minor (any person younger than 18

22 https://2001-2009.state.gov/g/drl/rls/hrrpt/2005/61718.htm

23 https://www.rollingstone.com/culture/culture-news/the-world-cup-of-
dirty-dreams-inside-brazils-most-infamous-brothel-57314/

years old) is sanctioned criminally.[24] Engaging in prostitution with a minor in Brazil can subject a person to up to 10 years in jail.

The age of consent for sexual activity in Brazil is 14 years of age. However, for purposes of prostitution, a sex worker cannot legally grant consent until they are at least 18 years old.

 **Legality and Penalties**

Although prostitution is legal, the associated regulatory framework complicates the landscape for sex workers, leaving them without formal recognition or labor protections. This lack of legal support makes them susceptible to exploitation and penalties under public order laws, while stringent regulations address the exploitation of minors, solicitation, and the challenges of child and adolescent prostitution. Prostitution typically takes place in public areas, especially nightlife districts, yet enforcement of laws often results in harassment of sex workers rather than the creation of safe zones.

While adult sex workers do not need to register or obtain licenses, they face restrictions regarding brothels and pimping, which are illegal activities punishable by significant prison terms, ranging from two to five years, depending on the severity of the offense. These workers frequently operate without labor rights, increasing their vulnerability to violence and exploitation. Despite advocacy for improved safety measures and health checks, the absence of a structured legal approach complicates their conditions. The legal framework primarily targets sex workers instead of addressing the root causes of exploitation, perpetuating their precarious status within society.[25]

---

24 https://web.archive.org/web/20160313000246/http://www.planalto.gov.br/ccivil_03/decreto-lei/Del2848compilado.htm

25 https://en.wikipedia.org/wiki/Prostitution_in_Brazil

Prostitution Practices

In Brazil, prostitution is a legally acknowledged profession with approximately 1.2 million individuals involved, most of whom are women operating primarily in urban nightlife districts. However, the environment is fraught with challenges, including a higher prevalence of HIV among female sex workers, estimated at 5.3 percent, and significant exposure to violence, with around 40 percent reporting such experiences.[26]

Child and adolescent prostitution is also a critical issue, with thousands of minors being exploited, prompting stringent laws aimed at combating this problem. These statistics highlight the complexities and vulnerabilities faced by sex workers in Brazil, underscoring the urgent need for protective measures and legal reforms.

Prostitution in Brazil takes various forms, including street prostitution, brothel work, escort services, and online sex work, each presenting unique challenges for those involved. Street prostitution is the most visible, with sex workers soliciting clients in public areas, often facing risks such as harassment and violence. Brothels remain prevalent despite being illegal, providing venues where workers may be exploited and lack legal protections. Escort services have seen growth through online platforms, allowing workers more independence, but also exposing them to safety risks. Meanwhile, online sex work allows for anonymity and control over earnings, yet it also comes with potential harassment and exploitation.

While prostitution is legal in Brazil, local authorities tend to adopt a repressive approach, focusing on policing sex work rather than protecting workers' rights and safety. Street-based sex workers face harassment and legal penalties, exacerbating their vulnerability. While some advocacy groups push for better health and safety measures, authorities often intervene without consulting sex workers and proposed reforms face resistance and lack legislative support.[27]

---

26 https://pmc.ncbi.nlm.nih.gov/articles/PMC5991538/

27 https://sxpolitics.org/around-the-world-306/8505

Sex Trafficking and Exploitation

Sex trafficking and exploitation in Brazil present significant societal and legal challenges, deeply rooted in socio-economic vulnerabilities and systemic issues. The country is a notable source, transit, and destination for sex trafficking, exacerbated by high poverty rates, economic instability, and political crises, particularly following the COVID-19 pandemic, which further intensified these vulnerabilities.[28]

Vulnerable populations including women, children, and LGBTQ individuals are disproportionately affected, often lured into trafficking through false job promises and deception by traffickers. Reports indicate that child prostitution remains a critical issue, with thousands of minors being exploited, further intensifying the urgency for effective interventions and legal redress.[29]

The response from Brazilian authorities has been complex and often inadequate, primarily targeting the actions surrounding sex work rather than addressing the underlying causes of trafficking and exploitation. Law enforcement frequently employs punitive measures that fail to provide protection for victims and, instead, criminalize the very individuals they are meant to help. Despite some positive initiatives aimed at combating trafficking, such as the establishment of anti-trafficking units and increased cooperation with international organizations, the overarching legal framework lacks comprehensive support for victims. Advocates argue that a shift toward recognizing and empowering sex workers, alongside dismantling the stigmas surrounding sex work, is essential to creating a safer and more just environment for vulnerable populations in Brazil.

---

28 https://www.unodc.org/unodc/en/news/2024/August/new-plan-to-combat-human-trafficking-launched-in-brazil.html

29 https://humanrights.stanford.edu/sites/humanrights/files/domestic_child_trafficking_brazil_dolby_final_report.pdf

Vulnerable Areas and Demographics

Certain areas in Brazil are more vulnerable to sex trafficking due to factors such as high tourism, poverty, and weak law enforcement. Major cities like São Paulo and Rio de Janeiro, along with tourist destinations such as Fortaleza and Salvador, are particularly at risk, especially during large events like Carnival. Border regions, such as Roraima and Acre, are also vulnerable due to cross-border trafficking, particularly with migrants from countries like Venezuela. Rural and isolated areas, as well as regions with indigenous populations, are also targeted due to limited access to social services and heightened isolation.

The most vulnerable demographics in Brazil include children and adolescents, especially girls and teenagers, who are often lured by traffickers with promises of a better life. Women and girls from low-income or marginalized backgrounds are also at high risk due to poverty and social inequality. Migrants, particularly Venezuelan refugees and others from economically unstable regions, are increasingly exploited by traffickers. Additionally, indigenous women and children, as well as transgender individuals, face heightened risks due to social exclusion, discrimination, and limited access to legal protections. Street children in urban areas are another group highly susceptible to trafficking.

 ## Sex Tourism and Public Implications

Brazil is widely recognized as a prominent destination for sex tourism, fueled by its vibrant culture, popular events like Carnival, the FIFA World Cup, and the Olympics. Major cities such as Rio de Janeiro, São Paulo, Salvador, and Fortaleza draw large numbers of tourists, some of whom engage in sex tourism. Economic vulnerabilities, particularly in impoverished and rural areas, contribute to the exploitation of women, children, and marginalized groups. Although prostitution is legal in Brazil, child sex trafficking and exploitation are illegal but remain prevalent.

The Brazilian government has taken steps to combat sex tourism through awareness campaigns and stricter laws, but challenges remain, particularly in poverty-stricken areas. The industry raises ethical and public health concerns, including the spread of STIs like HIV/AIDS and the exploitation of vulnerable populations. Mental health issues, such as trauma and substance abuse, further complicate the situation. While improved healthcare and public health efforts are needed, sex tourism continues to be a persistent challenge in Brazil.

 **Tips to Avoid Being Solicited**

When traveling in Brazil, especially in popular tourist areas, you may encounter sex workers trying to engage you in conversation or offer services. While it's important to be respectful and polite, there are also strategies to help you avoid being hassled. Here are some practical tips to avoid unwanted attention from sex workers:

- **Be aware of your surroundings but avoid eye contact:** If you're in areas known for sex work, like certain nightlife districts, you may be approached more frequently. Sex workers may approach you more often if they think you're showing interest, even unintentionally. Avoid making prolonged eye contact, as this can be interpreted as interest.

- **Polite but firm responses:** Say "Não, obrigado." (No, thank you). This is a clear, polite, but firm way to decline an offer.

- **Don't engage in conversation:** If you don't want to be hassled, avoid getting into any conversation or discussion. Simply and politely saying "no" or continuing to walk away is usually effective.

- **Avoid flashing money or valuables:** If you carry visible cash, expensive jewelry, or other valuables, you might attract more attention.

- **Travel in pairs or groups and avoid secluded or dark places:** Sex workers may target tourists in less trafficked, dimly lit areas. Stick to well-lit, populated streets.

- **Report persistent harassment:** If you're being persistently harassed by anyone, including sex workers, and it feels uncomfortable or threatening, you can contact the local police or authorities.

- **Research your destinations:** Before heading out, use apps or maps to familiarize yourself with the safest routes and areas where you're less likely to encounter aggressive solicitation.

 ## General Questions

1. *How does the absence of municipal laws regulating prostitution zones in Brazil affect the safety and working conditions of sex workers?* The absence of municipal laws regulating prostitution zones in Brazil leaves sex workers vulnerable, as they often operate in public areas like nightlife districts or streets. This exposes them to violence, harassment, and legal penalties. Without designated safe zones, they have limited protections, and local authorities focus more on enforcing public order laws than ensuring safety or rights, making sex workers more marginalized and at risk.

2. *What challenges do authorities in Brazil face when trying to address prostitution and sex trafficking, particularly in rural or less populated areas?* One of the primary challenges Brazil faces in combating prostitution and sex trafficking, especially in rural or less populated areas, is the lack of resources and awareness among local authorities. In these regions, poverty, lack of education, and economic hardship often make young girls and women more vulnerable to exploitation by traffickers. The isolation of rural areas also complicates the detection of trafficking activities and the rescue of victims.

Another challenge is the social normalization of prostitution in certain areas, where it may be seen as a viable option for economic survival, making it harder to change attitudes and protect vulnerable individuals. The absence of strong policing and legal infrastructure in these areas means traffickers often operate with little interference.

3. *What role do international organizations play in combating sex trafficking and prostitution-related exploitation in Brazil?* International organizations like UNICEF, INTERPOL, and the International Organization for Migration (IOM) play a key role in combating sex trafficking and exploitation in Brazil. They provide training for law enforcement, offer funding for victim support programs, and facilitate international cooperation to disrupt trafficking networks. These organizations also help raise awareness about child sex tourism and assist in the rehabilitation of survivors. While their efforts are crucial, challenges such as limited resources and political resistance can sometimes hinder progress.

 **Law of the Land Hypothetical**

HYPOTHETICAL: *David, a tourist from the U.S., is visiting the vibrant city of Rio de Janeiro. While exploring the nightlife in the Lapa district, a known area for bars and clubs, he finds himself approached by several individuals offering various services. He's feeling uncomfortable but doesn't want to be rude. What is the best way for David to handle the situation respectfully and avoid further attention, based on the tips to avoid unwanted solicitation in Brazil?*

ANSWER: *David should stay calm and avoid making prolonged eye contact, especially in areas like Lapa, where it might be misinterpreted as interest. If approached, he should politely but firmly say "Não, obrigado" (No, thank you) and avoid engaging in conversation. He should stay aware of his surroundings, avoiding dimly lit or less crowded areas, and consider traveling with a friend or in a group for added safety. If the harassment becomes persistent or threatening, David should contact local authorities for assistance.*

CHAPTER 8
LGBTQ

LGBTQ

Homophobia in Brazil[30]

Brazil exhibits a complex and evolving stance on homosexuality, marked by significant legislative advancements and a shifting societal attitude. On one hand, Brazil is recognized for its progressive legal frameworks regarding LGBTQ rights, being one of the first countries in Latin America to legalize same-sex marriage in 2013 and allowing adoption by same-sex couples. Research indicates that public acceptance has risen substantively, with a 2022 survey revealing that 79 percent of Brazilians believe homosexuality should be accepted by society.[31] This growing tolerance reflects a broader cultural shift that challenges traditional views.

Conversely, despite these advancements, Brazil continues to grapple with severe anti-LGBTQ violence and discrimination. Reports show that Brazil has one of the highest rates of murder against LGBTQ individuals, particularly targeting transgender women.[32] This reality presents a stark contrast to the country's legal progress, highlighting ongoing societal resistance rooted in deeply entrenched machismo and conservative beliefs. Consequently, while Brazil's legal environment for LGBTQ rights is relatively liberal, the persistent violence and discrimination against

---

30 https://www.equaldex.com/region/brazil

31 https://en.wikipedia.org/wiki/LGBTQ_rights_in_Brazil

32 https://www.statista.com/statistics/1319582/
    brasil-public-opinion-same-sex-marriage-by-age

sexual minorities illustrate that the journey toward true societal acceptance remains fraught with challenges.

LGBTQ Legislation

LGBTQ rights in Brazil are among the most progressive in Latin
America, with nationwide marriage equality since 2013, and a 2019
Supreme Court ruling making discrimination based on sexual orientation and gender identity a crime. In 2011, the Supreme Court granted same-sex couples equal legal rights, and in 2018, it allowed gender
identity changes on official documents without surgery. Despite these
legal advancements, Brazil faces high levels of discrimination and violence against LGBTQ individuals, with 316 violent deaths in 2021 alone.
Contributing factors include deep social conservatism, a hostile political
climate, and inadequate protective measures in many states, exacerbated
by underreporting of violence.

LGBTQ Tourism and Safety Concerns

Brazil is often recognized as one of the top destinations for LGBTQ travelers, particularly due to its world-renowned events like the São Paulo
Gay Pride Parade, which attracts millions and generates substantial economic benefits for the city. Furthermore, cities such as Rio de Janeiro,
São Paulo, and Florianópolis offer a plethora of gay-friendly accommodations, venues, and attractions, making them appealing choices for
LGBTQ tourists seeking welcoming environments (https://www.mis-
terbandb.com/gay-guide/brazil). The tourism sector has increasingly
catered to LGBTQ consumers, with approximately 26 percent of visitors
to major Brazilian cities identifying as part of the LGBTQ community.[33]

Urban hubs such as Rio de Janeiro and São Paulo are celebrated for
their LGBTQ-friendly atmospheres, while the northern and north-
eastern regions, traditionally among Brazil's poorest, often exhibit less
tolerance and are shaped by conservative values deeply embedded in

---

33 https://en.wikipedia.org/wiki/LGBTQ_tourism_in_Brazil

cultural traditions. Concurrently, attitudes toward public displays of affection for LGBTQ+ individuals are inconsistent across the country. In larger cities, there is an overall acceptance of LGBTQ+ PDA, particularly in supportive neighborhoods and during significant events such as Pride parades. In these urban contexts, affectionate gestures, including hand-holding and kissing, are commonplace and embraced as part of everyday life. Conversely, in smaller towns and rural areas, more conservative attitudes dominate, where LGBTQ+ individuals may encounter disapproving stares or verbal criticisms for showcasing PDA. In such places, it is advisable for LGBTQ+ visitors to be cautious and considerate of local cultural values.

Safety Tips for LGBTQ Travelers

LGBTQ travelers heading to Brazil can enjoy a vibrant culture and welcoming environments, however, to ensure a safe and enjoyable experience, it's essential to keep a few tips in mind:

- **Research Your Destination:** Before traveling, familiarize yourself with the specific LGBTQ climate in the areas you plan to visit.

- **Choose LGBTQ-Friendly Accommodations:** Select hotels that are recognized as LGBTQ-friendly. Many establishments in urban centers cater specifically to the LGBTQ community and offer a supportive environment.

- **Be Mindful of Public Displays of Affection:** While PDA is generally accepted in larger cities, exercising discretion in rural areas is advisable. In cities, openly affectionate gestures are commonly accepted.

- **Connect with Local LGBTQ Organizations:** Engage with local LGBTQ groups or resources that can provide valuable insights and support. They often host events and have recommendations for safe spaces.

- **Use Caution in Less Tolerant Areas:** In regions with conservative values, maintain a level of awareness about your surroundings and consider being less visibly affectionate or public in showcases of your identity.

- **Stay Updated on Safety Concerns:** Stay informed on local news and reports related to LGBTQ safety in Brazil. Community protection and awareness of rising concerns regarding discrimination or violence can enhance your experience.

- **Participate in LGBTQ Events:** Engaging in LGBTQ events, such as Pride parades or festivals, not only allows you to celebrate openly but also connects you with like-minded individuals.

- **Respect Local Culture:** While Brazil has made significant advances in LGBTQ rights, respecting cultural traditions and local customs can foster positive interactions and experiences.

 ## Law of the Land True Story[34]

High Profile Case: The Murder of Heleno Veggi Dumba. One significant case that highlights the ongoing violence against LGBTQ individuals in Brazil is the murder of Heleno Veggi Dumba, a gay doctor found dead in April 2024. Dumba, a gay man, was tragically shot in the head after being lured into an ambush via a dating app, highlighting the dangers LGBTQ individuals face, particularly those using such platforms. His death is part of a disturbing trend, with at least five gay men killed since March 2024 in similar circumstances. Legal experts argue these killings reflect broader structural homophobia, with criminals exploiting the victims' reluctance to report incidents due to fear of discrimination and mistrust of law enforcement. Following Dumba's murder, advocacy groups have called for stronger protections and improved investigations to address the violence against LGBTQ people. While three suspects have been arrested, the case underscores the ongoing risks to the LGBTQ community in Brazil and the need for systemic societal change.

---

34 https://www.nbcnews.com/nbc-out/out-news/
gay-brazilians-targeted-deadly-stickups-lured-dating-apps-rcna168205

 **Law of the Land Hypothetical**

HYPOTHETICAL: *Juliana and Mariana, a same-sex couple from Colombia, decide to marry in Brazil, one of the few Latin American countries where same-sex marriage is legal. They plan to honeymoon in Rio de Janeiro and are excited about their wedding. After arriving, they visit the civil registry office in Rio, where they're informed there are some legal requirements they have to meet. What is the one legal requirement for Juliana and Mariana to be able to marry in Brazil, and what rights do they have as a same-sex couple?*

ANSWER: *Juliana and Mariana must meet the residency requirement, meaning one of them needs to live in Brazil for at least 30 days. After fulfilling this, they can marry legally. Their marriage grants them the same rights as any married couple, such as inheritance, property rights, and tax benefits, along with legal protection against discrimination based on sexual orientation.*

SEXUALLY MOTIVATED/ VIOLENT CRIMES

SEXUALLY MOTIVATED/ VIOLENT CRIMES

Overview[35]

Brazil faces a pervasive issue with sexually violent crimes, marked by alarming statistics and social repercussions. In recent years, the country has witnessed a significant rise in reported cases of sexual violence, with a disturbing average of one rape occurring every six minutes in 2023. This equated to approximately 83,988 incidents for the year, reflecting a 6.5 percent increase from the previous year. The Brazilian Public Security Forum indicates that the numbers may be even higher due to the underreporting of such crimes, as many victims do not come forward due to fear, stigma, or a lack of trust in authorities.[36]

Sexually violent crimes in Brazil predominantly affect women and children, with women making up over 86 percent of victims.[37] Femicide— the killing of women based on their gender—is also a concerning facet of this issue, with many cases linked to intimate partner violence and

---

35 https://www.genocidewatch.com/single-post/
    violence-against-women-in-brazil-reaches-highest-levels-on-record

36 https://www.ohchr.org/en/news/2024/05/experts-committee-elimina-
    tion-discrimination-against-women-praise-brazils-maria-da

37 https://www.statista.com/statistics/1172704/
    rape-sexual-assault-cases-gender-brazil/

societal misogyny. Children are particularly vulnerable, as data suggests that around 61 percent of reported rape cases involve minors, and a notable percentage of these incidents involve familial relationships, with perpetrators often being known to the victims.[38]

In response to this crisis, Brazil has implemented various legal frameworks to address sexual violence, notably the Maria da Penha Law, enacted in 2006 to combat domestic violence and provide greater protection for women. However, enforcement remains inconsistent, and many victims report a lack of effective support from law enforcement and social services, further complicating the fight against sexual violence.

Public awareness and advocacy groups have been crucial in raising the profile of these issues, often pressing for better legal protections and support systems for victims. Activism has underscored the need for more comprehensive educational programs addressing gender-based violence and the importance of societal change to combat the deeply rooted cultural norms that perpetuate these crimes.

Related Legislation[39]

Brazil has enacted a series of legal measures aimed at combating sexually violent crimes, with a particular focus on protecting women and children. One of the cornerstone regulations is the Maria da Penha Law, established in 2006, which specifically targets domestic violence and offers a range of protective measures for victims of gender-based violence. This law not only provides for increased penalties for offenders but also establishes special courts to expedite cases of domestic violence,

---

38 https://brazilreports.com/
    in-brazil-8-people-are-raped-every-hour-study/5110/

39 https://www.omct.org/files/2004/07/2409/eng_2003_02_brazil.pd-
    f#:~:text=Articles%20213%2C%20215%2C%20216%20and%20217%20
    deal,period%20of%206%20up%20to%2010%20years.

ensuring a more focused judicial response to such incidents.[40] The effective implementation of the Maria da Penha Law has been vital in raising awareness of women's rights and addressing the broader issues of sexual violence within the domestic sphere.

In terms of penalties, the Brazilian Penal Code outlines severe consequences for various forms of sexual violence. For instance, the crime of rape, defined as coercing someone through violence or serious threat to engage in sexual acts, carries a punishment of six to thirty years of imprisonment. Furthermore, sexual harassment, which is treated as a distinct crime, also incurs significant penalties under the law, ranging from one to five years of imprisonment depending on the circumstances and severity of the offense.

General Questions

1. *Do laws in Brazil related to sex crimes protect the victims equally?* **No.** Laws in Brazil related to sex crimes provide frameworks aimed at protecting victims; however, they do not always ensure equal protection for all individuals. Vulnerable populations, particularly women and LGBTQ individuals, often face additional barriers in seeking justice due to societal stigma, systemic discrimination, and inefficient law enforcement practices, which can hinder the equitable application of these laws. Consequently, while legislative measures exist, gaps in enforcement and societal attitudes can result in unequal protection for victims of sex crimes.

---

40 https://resourcehub.bakermckenzie.com/en/resources/fighting-domestic-violence/latin-america-and-the-caribbean/brazil/topics/1legal-provisions

2. ***Pursuant to law, what is the age of consent for sex in Brazil?*** In Brazil, the age of consent is set at 14 years, regardless of gender or sexual orientation. There are judicial precedents that allow for close-in-age exceptions for individuals aged 12 to 13 to engage in sexual activity with partners who are up to five years older.[41]

 **Law of the Land Hypothetical**

In Brazil, Raul can be charged with rape if he uses physical force or intimidates someone into engaging in sexual relations. Physical violence is not required for this charge; the mere threat of violence is enough to accuse Raul of rape. Once charged, Raul would not be eligible for bail, and he would remain in jail until his trial. Brazilian prosecutors take this charge very seriously due to the exponential increase in this type of crime in recent years. Raul can expect the local authorities to vigorously prosecute this type of crime. Raul should seek assistance from his embassy and hire a local attorney to ensure a proper legal defense.

---

41   https://en.wikipedia.org/wiki/Age_of_consent_in_South_America

ARRESTED IN BRAZIL

CHAPTER 10

ARRESTED IN BRAZIL

Overview

When traveling in a foreign country, it is imperative to recognize that you are subject to the legal jurisdiction and regulations of that country. These laws may significantly differ from those in your home country and might not offer the same legal protections you are accustomed to. It is crucial to bear in mind that penalties for violating foreign laws can be more severe than those for similar offenses in your home country, and ignorance of these laws is not typically accepted as a defense.

The consequences for breaking the law while abroad can be severe and may include expulsion, fines, arrest, or imprisonment. Even unintentional violations can lead to serious legal repercussions. It is essential for travelers to be aware of and adhere to the laws of the host country to avoid legal entanglements and ensure a safe and enjoyable experience.

Specifically, stringent penalties are often enforced for possession, use, or trafficking of illegal drugs in many countries. Convicted offenders can expect severe consequences, including lengthy jail sentences and hefty fines. The legal processes for foreigners in the event of an arrest abroad involve being charged or indicted, prosecuted, potentially convicted and sentenced, and, if applicable, going through an appeals process.

Navigating a foreign legal system can be complex, and individuals arrested abroad must be prepared to comply with the legal procedures of the host country. Seeking legal representation and understanding the local legal nuances are crucial steps for those facing legal issues in a foreign jurisdiction.

Arrested Process

Brazilian criminal law encompasses a wide range of offenses, reflecting the country's social complexities and varying crime rates. Among the most prevalent criminal charges are homicide and related crimes, including femicide. The Brazilian homicide rate remains alarmingly high, with reports indicating a sharp increase in intentional killings in recent years. Other serious offenses linked to violence include aggravated assault, robbery, and drug trafficking, with drug-related crimes forming a substantial part of the country's organized crime landscape.

In addition to violent crimes, Brazil faces challenges with financial and white-collar crimes, notably tax evasion and corruption. Corruption has been a persistent issue, especially within governmental and public institutions, leading to significant legal repercussions for politicians and public officials. The Brazilian Penal Code also addresses crimes such as domestic violence, sexual violence—including rape and harassment—and child exploitation, which disproportionately affect women and vulnerable populations.

Rights of the Arrested Person

In Brazil, the constitution guarantees that no one can be deprived of liberty without legal justification. Article 5 mandates a judicial warrant for arrests, which means that law enforcement must present evidence to a judge before an arrest. If a suspect is apprehended in flagrante delicto (in the act of committing a crime), they must be informed of their rights, including the right to remain silent and the right to legal counsel. Authorities must present the detainee before a judge within 24 hours for a legality review.

During the judicial review, the judge may ratify the arrest, release the individual if unlawful, or grant provisional detention for further investigation. In some cases, precautionary measures like temporary detention may be imposed, adhering to constitutional rights. If charges are filed, the pretrial phase begins, where evidence is presented and legal arguments are made. Defendants retain the right to challenge evidence and confront witnesses.

The trial process includes a pleading stage, an evidentiary stage, and a decision-making phase, all respecting due process rights, including legal counsel, a fair trial, and access to evidence. Sentencing follows the Brazilian Penal Code, with penalties including imprisonment, fines, or community service. Judges consider aggravating and mitigating factors when determining sentences, with a maximum prison term of 30 years for serious crimes like homicide, preventing cumulative sentences from exceeding this limit.

Brazil promotes alternative dispute resolution to reduce court congestion. They also accommodate special provisions for juvenile offenders and recognize the importance of rehabilitation, reflecting a growing trend toward more humane sentencing practices.

Getting Legal Assistance

Foreign nationals arrested in Brazil are afforded a range of rights designed to protect their legal standing and ensure fair treatment within the justice system. Central to these rights is the provision outlined in the Brazilian Constitution and the Vienna Convention on Consular Relations, which mandates all detainees be informed of their rights promptly upon arrest. This includes the critical right to consular access, whereby foreign nationals can contact their home country's embassy or consulate for assistance.[42]

In addition to consular access, foreign nationals in Brazil are guaranteed the right to legal representation. If they cannot afford an attorney, the

---

42 https://travel.state.gov/content/travel/en/consularnotification.html

state is obligated to provide free legal assistance to ensure they can effectively navigate the judicial process. Furthermore, the Brazilian legal system requires that foreign detainees be treated in accordance with international human rights standards, which encompasses access to adequate medical care and humane treatment while in custody. The Constitution also prohibits arbitrary detention, ensuring that arrests are conducted legally, with the necessity of a judicial warrant unless the individual is caught committing a crime in plain view. The country also participates in international treaties concerning the transfer of sentenced persons, enabling foreign nationals to serve their sentences in their home countries. However, challenges such as language barriers and varying treatment standards in prisons can complicate their experiences.

Despite these protections, the actual implementation of these rights can be inconsistent, highlighting the need for ongoing efforts to uphold the principles of justice for all individuals, including foreign nationals, within Brazil's legal framework.

Role of Home Embassy and Consulate

Your home embassy or consulate can offer crucial support, such as legal guidance, translation services, and communication with family members. They can also visit the detained U.S. citizen in jail, help ensure that prison officials provide appropriate medical care, explain the local criminal justice and legal processes, and most importantly, connect you to local attorneys who speak English. However, bear in mind, their powers are limited, and they cannot get U.S. citizens out of jail, provide legal advice or represent U.S. citizens in court, serve as official interpreters or translators, nor can they pay your legal, medical, or other fees.

The United States maintains a significant diplomatic presence in Brazil, encompassing one embassy and five consulates across the country. Specifically, the U.S. Embassy is located in Brasília, while consulates can be found in São Paulo, Rio de Janeiro, Porto Alegre, and Recife. For contact information on each, please visit **https://br.usembassy.gov/**.

The Department of State provides a list of English-speaking attorneys in Brazil; however, it does not assume responsibility or liability for the qualifications, reputation, or quality of services provided by the listed entities or individual. The information is provided directly by the service providers, and the Department cannot verify its accuracy.

 You can find a list of English-speaking attorneys in Brazil at **https://br.usembassy.gov/2018-ylai-participants/ legal-assistence/**

Bail

In Brazil, the bail system is not as commonly used as in some other countries, such as the United States. Instead, Brazil operates under a system that focuses more on preventive detention, where individuals accused of certain crimes are often detained before trial, depending on the severity of the offense, flight risk, or risk to public safety.

Here's a breakdown of how the system works:

1. **Preventive Detention:** Under Brazilian law, a person can be held in preventive detention if there is a risk of them fleeing, interfering with the investigation, or committing further crimes. This is more common for serious crimes, including violent offenses, drug trafficking, or organized crime.

2. **No Bail for Serious Crimes:** In Brazil, the legal system generally does not allow bail for individuals accused of serious crimes, such as murder, rape, or organized crime. These individuals are likely to be detained until their trial, unless a judge decides there is a strong case for their release under certain conditions.

3. **Release with Conditions:** For less serious crimes, a judge may allow an individual to be released with certain conditions, such as surrendering their passport, regular check-ins with the police, or staying within a certain geographic area. However, the concept of bail in the sense of a financial deposit to secure release is not commonly used.

4. **Release Pending Trial:** If an individual is accused of a less serious crime, they may be granted temporary release while awaiting trial, but this is often conditional and depends on factors like the nature of the crime, the risk of reoffending, and whether the individual has a criminal record.

5. **Judicial Discretion:** The decision to grant or deny bail (or conditional release) is ultimately up to the judge's discretion. They will consider factors such as the individual's ties to the community, employment status, and the risk of them fleeing before trial.

6. **Length of Pretrial Detention:** Brazil has faced criticism for the long periods of pretrial detention, where people may be held in prison for extended periods, sometimes for years, before a trial even takes place. This has led to calls for reform in the judicial system.

Complaints Against Police

The reputation of the Brazilian police force is complex and varies widely across the country. While many officers are dedicated and professional, the force as a whole faces significant criticism for issues such as corruption, excessive use of force, and human rights violations. The police are often accused of being involved in illegal activities like bribery and extortion, particularly in areas where organized crime is prevalent. One of the most common complaints is the use of excessive violence, especially in urban centers and *favelas* (shanty town or slum), where police often resort to heavy-handed tactics, including extrajudicial killings. Racial profiling is another major concern, with Afro-Brazilian communities disproportionately targeted and subjected to discriminatory treatment.

Additionally, there are frequent reports of a lack of proper training in human rights and conflict resolution, leading to confrontations that escalate unnecessarily. The militarization of the police has also been criticized, as military-style tactics often treat civilians as adversaries rather than as individuals to protect. The police force is also accused of weak accountability mechanisms, with officers rarely being held responsible for misconduct. This lack of accountability, combined with allegations of police involvement with criminal organizations, contributes to the public's lack of trust in the police, particularly in marginalized communities.

Filing a Complaint Against Police

To file a complaint against a police officer in Brazil, individuals should follow several key steps to ensure proper documentation and processing. Initially, it is important to gather all relevant information about the incident, including the date, time, location, a description of the events, and identification of the involved officers if possible. This information establishes the context and substantiates the claims.

Next, individuals must identify the appropriate agency to submit their complaint. In Brazil, complaints can be directed to the relevant police department, the municipality's Ombudsman's Office, or the Ministry of Human Rights and Citizenship. Various police departments often have specific channels for processing such complaints. After determining the appropriate agency, individuals can initiate their complaints in person, via email, or through online platforms, adhering to the agency's specific procedures. It is crucial to complete any necessary forms and include detailed information, along with supporting evidence like photographs, videos, or witness statements, while retaining copies for personal records.

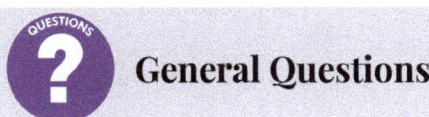

General Questions

1. *If I am convicted in Brazil, am I likely to be released on bail pending the outcome of my appeal?* In Brazil, release on bail pending an appeal is not common and depends on the crime. For serious offenses, such as violent crimes or drug trafficking, bail is less likely. Temporary release may be granted if the person is not considered a flight risk or danger to society, but this is at the judge's discretion. For many cases, especially severe crimes, individuals are kept in custody during the appeal process.

2. *What influences a bail determination?* A judge's decision to grant bail is influenced by several factors, including the severity of the crime, the likelihood of the defendant fleeing, and the risk posed to society. Other considerations include the defendant's criminal record, whether they are a repeat offender, and whether they have strong ties to the community, such as family or employment. For serious crimes like homicide or drug trafficking, bail is often denied, while for less serious offenses, the judge may grant temporary release if the defendant is not seen as a flight risk or threat.

3. *Who is entitled to bail?* In Brazil, individuals charged with less serious offenses are generally more likely to be granted bail, especially if they are not considered a flight risk or a danger to society. Factors such as a lack of a criminal record, strong community ties, and the nature of the offense influence the decision. For serious crimes, such as homicide or organized crime, bail is often denied. Ultimately, the decision is based on the severity of the crime, the risk posed by the defendant, and their ties to the community.

4. *If I am arrested, how soon will I see a judge or magistrate?* In Brazil, if you are arrested, you are required by law to be brought before a judge or magistrate within 24 hours of your arrest. The judge will then determine whether the arrest was lawful and decide whether to grant bail, impose preventive detention, or release you, depending on the circumstances. If the arrest was made under suspicion (without a warrant), the judge will review the case and assess the evidence to determine if detention is justified. If you're arrested for a more serious crime, detention may be ordered, but if it's a minor offense, you might be granted release with conditions.

5. *Will I be able to contact my country's embassy in Brazil?* Yes, if you are arrested in Brazil, you have the right to contact your country's embassy or consulate. Under international law, Brazil is obligated to inform foreign nationals of their right to communicate with their embassy. The embassy can provide assistance, including helping you find legal representation, ensuring your

rights are respected, and offering support throughout the legal process.

 ## Law of the Land Hypothetical

HYPOTHETICAL: *Raul, a foreigner arrested in Brazil for possessing large quantities of cocaine, is facing charges likely related to drug trafficking. He is informed that prosecutors have 45 days to file formal charges, though this period may be extended due to backlogs. As Raul's arrest was based on witness statements, the 45-day timeline applies. Concerned about his detention, Raul wonders about his chances of bail, knowing Brazil's strict approach to drug charges. Given the seriousness of his case, he fears a lengthy stay in pre-trial detention and is uncertain if he'll be granted bail before trial.*

Can Raul request bail, and if so, how likely is he to be granted bail in Brazil, considering the severity of his crime and the legal framework surrounding bail?

ANSWER: *Raul can request bail from a judge at any point, but chances are low for serious crimes like drug trafficking. Brazilian judges typically deny bail for such offenses due to concerns over public safety and flight risk. To improve his chances, Raul should consult a local attorney and present factors like his intent to stay in Brazil, community ties, or lack of a criminal record.*

If bail is denied, Raul could remain in pre-trial detention for up to 120 days, though delays are possible. If convicted and sentenced to over 20 years, he can request a re-trial. Raul is entitled to consular assistance and, if unable to afford an attorney, a public defender will be appointed.

JAILS VS. PRISONS: CONDITIONS & CULTURE

JAILS VS. PRISONS: CONDITIONS & CULTURE

Overview

In Brazil, jails and prisons serve distinct purposes within the criminal justice system. The primary function of **jails**, known as *"delegacias"* or *"cárceres,"* is as detention centers for individuals awaiting trial or those sentenced to short-term confinement (up to three years) for minor offenses. They focus on temporarily holding suspects and may experience issues of overcrowding, often leading to delays in judicial processes.

On the other hand, **prisons**, referred to as *"prisões"* or *"penitenciárias,"* are designed for the long-term incarceration of individuals convicted of serious crimes. Their primary purpose is punishment and rehabilitation, with an emphasis on facilitating educational and vocational programs for inmates. However, Brazilian prisons face several challenges, most prevalent being severe overcrowding in facilities designed for far fewer, resulting in cramped conditions, insufficient sanitation, and inadequate nutrition. This overcrowding exacerbates violence among inmates and fuels gang activity. In addition to overcrowding, inhumane living conditions are rampant, including widespread torture, psychological abuse, and neglect of basic hygiene and healthcare. These deficiencies lead to health crises, the spread of diseases, and preventable deaths.[43]

---

43 https://www.conectas.org/en/noticias/
     mandela-rules-the-problems-of-the-brazilian-prison-system

Violence is another significant issue, with frequent riots, attacks, and killings, often driven by gang conflicts. The lack of proper inmate classification and the failure to address these issues contribute to further violence and hinder rehabilitation efforts. Although there are calls for reform, Brazil's penal system struggles with political indifference and a lack of resources for effective change. Advocates argue that addressing these problems requires legal reforms, increased funding, and a focus on human rights.

Prison Population

Brazil's prison population is predominantly young, male, black, and undereducated, with 89 percent of inmates lacking basic education. Women are the fastest-growing segment, with incarceration rates for females increasing by 10.7 percent annually between 2005 and 2014, a trend that continues. Theft and drug trafficking are the most common offenses, while homicides account for less than 20 percent of detainees.

Approximately 40 percent of prisoners are pre-trial detainees, with some regions, like Amazonas, seeing pre-trial detention rates exceed 70 percent. This is largely due to a shortage of public defenders and judges' reluctance to consider alternative sentences for non-violent offenses. Many pre-trial detainees are held with convicted prisoners, violating international and Brazilian standards.

Prison Conditions and Living Environment

Brazil's prison system is organized into three main types of regimes: closed, semi-open, and open, each designed for different categories of offenders.[44]

- The **closed regime** is the most restrictive, reserved for individuals convicted of serious crimes like violent offenses and organized crime. Inmates are kept in high-security facilities with limited contact with

---

44 https://www.hrw.org/legacy/reports98/brazil/Brazil-03.htm

the outside world, and strict surveillance is maintained to prevent escape and ensure safety.

- The **semi-open regime** is for inmates who show good behavior and have less severe sentences. These individuals are allowed to leave the facility during the day for work or education but must return at night. This regime focuses on rehabilitation and social reintegration.

- The **open regime** is the least restrictive and applies to those serving short sentences for less serious crimes. Inmates in open facilities have greater freedom and often participate in community service or other outside activities to aid their reintegration into society.

While these regimes are designed to address the diverse needs of inmates, challenges like overcrowding and violence persist, undermining the effectiveness of the system. Although the different security levels aim to tailor incarceration to the behavior and risk levels of inmates, Brazil's prison system continues to face significant operational and systemic issues.

Access to Healthcare in Prisons

Despite legal guarantees, healthcare in Brazilian prisons is severely lacking due to overcrowding, unsanitary conditions, and a shortage of qualified medical staff. Many prisons operate beyond capacity, creating an environment where infectious diseases like tuberculosis and HIV/AIDS thrive. Inadequate screening, insufficient medical supplies, and delays in treatment further worsen health outcomes for inmates. Often, prisoners rely on family members for medications due to the inefficiency of prison healthcare.

Mental healthcare is similarly inadequate, with a lack of psychiatrists, psychologists, and social workers to meet the needs of the incarcerated population. Despite legal requirements, many inmates with conditions like depression, anxiety, and psychosis receive little to no care. Substance abuse is another major issue, with underfunded and insufficient detox and rehabilitation programs that fail to address the scale of the problem. Stigma also discourages prisoners from seeking help.

Food, Sanitation, and Basic Needs[45]

Access to adequate food and sanitation in Brazilian prisons remains a significant human rights issue. Many prisons fail to provide sufficient or nutritious meals, with overcrowding exacerbating food insecurity. Inmates often receive minimal rations, and some powerful inmate groups manipulate food distribution, leaving weaker prisoners underserved. Many rely on their families for additional food, creating inequalities among inmates based on economic status.

Sanitation conditions are similarly poor, with overcrowded facilities lacking basic hygiene standards. Inmates face inadequate access to clean water, broken toilets, and unsanitary conditions that foster the spread of disease, including respiratory and skin infections. Personal hygiene is difficult to maintain due to a lack of soap and clean water, often requiring inmates to depend on family members or the prison commissary.

Basic necessities like clothing, bedding, and healthcare are also in short supply. Many prisoners, especially in colder months, lack adequate clothing and rely on external support. Despite international legal standards that mandate sufficient food, clean water, and hygiene, Brazil's prison system struggles to meet these essential needs, with limited resources and inadequate funding exacerbating the problem.

Inmate Rights and Legal Protections[46]

Inmates in Brazil are guaranteed several rights under the *Lei de Execução Penal* (Law of Execution of Sentences), including access to legal counsel, routine family visits, adequate medical care, access to educational materials, and the freedom to practice their religion. However, while these rights are enshrined in national law, inmates often face significant challenges in practice, such as overcrowding, poor living conditions, limited

---

45 https://www.hrw.org/legacy/reports98/brazil/Brazil-06.htm

46 https://www.hrw.org/legacy/reports98/brazil/Brazil-03.htm#:~:text=The%20most%20detailed%20statement%20of,community%20service%2C%20and%20suspended%20sentences

healthcare, and violence from both fellow inmates and prison staff. Rehabilitation programs, though mandated by law, are often scarce.

In terms of basic amenities, inmates have access to the commissary (or *"cantina"*), where they can purchase items like food, toiletries, and clothing using money sent by family or earnings from work programs. While these amenities provide some comfort, they are often limited by the prison's rules. Inmates in good behavior may also be eligible for work programs, which aim to provide skill development, social reintegration, and a small wage for purchases.

Family visitation is permitted but regulated, with rules varying by facility. Visits can be in person, through glass partitions, or via video calls in some modern prisons. Physical contact is typically restricted for security reasons, and all visitors are subject to security checks. Despite the availability of these amenities and rights, systemic issues such as overcrowding and violence continue to hinder the well-being and rehabilitation of prisoners in Brazil.

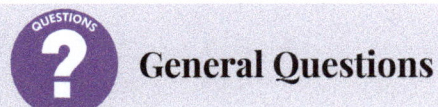

? General Questions

1. ***Do jails and prisons offer religious services to inmates?*** Yes, jails and prisons in Brazil generally offer religious services to inmates. Brazilian law guarantees prisoners the right to practice their religion, as long as it does not compromise safety or infringe on the rights of others. Religious services, including access to clergy, are available in many facilities, and inmates can participate in religious ceremonies, receive spiritual guidance, and engage in religious education. However, the quality and frequency of these services can vary depending on the facility and its resources

2. *How do prisoners spend their time?* In Brazilian prisons, inmates' routines depend on the facility and security level. Many participate in work programs, learning skills for rehabilitation, though wages are low. Educational opportunities are limited, and overcrowding restricts access. Some prisons offer recreational activities and religious services, but these are often scarce. Inmates receive visits from family and friends, with frequency depending on the facility. For those in high-security units, time is often spent in isolation, with minimal access to productive or social activities where poor conditions and overcrowding further limit opportunities for rehabilitation.

3. *What type of jobs can inmates perform?* In Brazilian prisons, inmates are assigned various types of work, depending on the available resources and the security level of the facility. These jobs often include tasks such as manufacturing goods, farming, maintenance work, kitchen duties, and laundry or housekeeping. The aim is to provide inmates with useful skills for reintegration into society. However, participation in these programs is usually conditional on good behavior, and the wages earned are minimal, primarily used for purchasing items from the prison commissary.

4. *How does the prison commissary system work in Brazil?* In Brazil's prisons, the commissary (cantina) allows inmates to buy food, toiletries, clothing, and other goods. Purchases are funded by family support or earnings from work programs. Access is regulated, with limits on spending and monitored by staff to prevent contraband. While it offers comfort, inmates without family support or work opportunities may have limited access to these resources.

5. ***What type of medical care do prisoners receive?*** In Brazilian prisons, inmates are entitled to medical care, but the quality and availability of services are often inadequate due to overcrowding and resource constraints. Basic healthcare is provided, including treatment for minor illnesses, injuries, and emergency care. However, access to specialized care, mental health services, and treatment for serious conditions can be limited. Many prisoners with chronic illnesses or complex medical needs struggle to receive timely or proper treatment. Medical care is often underfunded, and some prisons rely on outside support from NGOs (Non-Governmental Organizations) or family members to meet inmates' healthcare needs.

6. ***What is prison culture in Brazil?*** Prison culture in Brazil is shaped by overcrowding, violence, and powerful criminal gangs that control much of the prison environment. Inmates often form groups for protection, and violence between rival gangs is common. Poor living conditions and limited resources exacerbate these issues, while rehabilitation programs are often insufficient. The prison system is marked by a harsh survival mentality, with inmates navigating a complex social hierarchy.

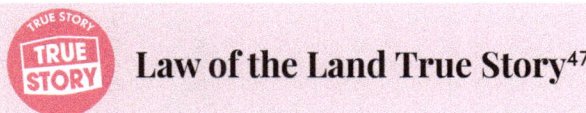 **Law of the Land True Story**[47]

Brazil Jail Riot In Para State Leaves 57 Dead As Gangs Fight. A prison riot in Altamira, Pará state, Brazil, left at least 57 people dead on July 29, 2019. The violence, which lasted five hours, involved a battle between rival gangs inside the overcrowded facility. Members of the Comando Classe A (CCA) gang attacked the Comando Vermelho (Red Command) gang by setting fire to their cell. The fire spread quickly, suffocating many prisoners, while 16 others were decapitated. Two

---

47   https://www.bbc.com/news/world-latin-america-49157858

prison officers were taken hostage but were later released, as the attackers focused on their rivals rather than the staff.

The Altamira jail, which has a capacity of 200, was holding 309 inmates at the time of the riot. Violence in Brazilian prisons is frequent, with overcrowding and gang warfare being major contributing factors. Brazil's prison system is plagued by poor conditions, underfunding, and limited resources, leading to frequent clashes and riots. This incident follows a long history of prison violence, including a similar outbreak in Manaus earlier in the year, and highlights the ongoing struggles of the Brazilian prison system.

The Brazilian government has pledged to tighten prison controls, but these efforts face significant challenges, particularly because prisons are managed at the state level.

HELPING A FRIEND OR RELATIVE IMPRISONED IN BRAZIL

HELPING A FRIEND OR RELATIVE IMPRISONED IN BRAZIL

 **Disclaimer:** The United States is referenced prominently throughout this section. However, this guideline is in general terms and is also applicable to citizens of other countries as well. For more information on assisting an inmate abroad, visit **https://br.usembassy.gov/u-s-citizen-services/arrest-of-a-u-s-citizen/**

 If someone you know has been arrested in Brazil, the first thing you should do is contact your home country's closest embassy or consulate to inform them of the situation.

Overview

Having a family member or friend imprisoned abroad, particularly in Brazil, can be a distressing and challenging experience. Navigating the legal and bureaucratic complexities of a foreign prison system can be daunting, but there are steps that can be taken to provide support and assistance:

1. **Understanding the Legal System:** The first step in supporting an imprisoned loved one in Brazil is to understand the local legal

system and the charges they face. Brazil's legal processes can differ greatly from other countries, so it's essential to consult a legal expert familiar with Brazilian criminal law. Local legal aid organizations may also offer assistance.

2. **Contacting the Embassy or Consulate:** Reach out to your home country's embassy or consulate in Brazil for support, including limited legal advice, guidance on local laws, and connections to criminal lawyers. The embassy can also facilitate communication with your loved one. The U.S. embassy, for example, provides a list of English-speaking attorneys on its website.

3. **Arranging Communication:** Regular communication is crucial. Most Brazilian prisons allow inmates to communicate via mail, phone, or visits. Be aware of monitoring and follow prison rules for correspondence and visitation. Establishing clear communication can provide emotional support and reduce feelings of isolation.

4. **Sending Care Packages and Financial Support:** If permitted, sending care packages with toiletries, clothing, and food can offer comfort. Providing financial support allows inmates to purchase necessities from the prison commissary. Familiarize yourself with the specific rules of the prison regarding care packages.

5. **Engaging with Non-Governmental Organizations (NGOs):** NGOs such as "Prisoners Abroad" and "Penal Reform International" offer support to prisoners, including human rights advocacy, legal help, and rehabilitation programs. Engaging with these organizations can provide additional resources and expert knowledge of the Brazilian prison system.

Sending Supplies and Money to an Inmate

Sending money and supplies to inmates in Brazilian prisons is a process involving strict regulations and guidelines. Families and friends can provide financial support to inmates through various methods, the most common being bank transfers or services like Western Union and Wise. While Western Union allows for direct cash transfers to inmates' accounts in Brazil, Wise offers competitive international transfer fees and favorable exchange rates, making it an appealing option for many senders.[48]

The U.S. Embassy can also help by setting up an Overseas Citizen's Trust, or OCS. OCS is a special account used to assist people in the United States that are sending money to friends or relatives abroad who are imprisoned or destitute. (If you have additional questions regarding the OCS Trust, call **202-647-5225**.) However, it is always vital to ensure that the correct recipient details are provided; this includes the inmate's full name and registration number, as inaccuracies can lead to delays or loss of funds.

In addition to monetary support, families may send supplies to inmates, though strict limits are imposed on what can be sent. Packages typically must be approved in advance, and only certain items are permissible, such as clothing, basic hygiene products, and legal materials.[49] Moreover, regulations often restrict the total value of items that can be sent in a care package, requiring that they do not exceed specific monetary limits. It is always advisable for those wishing to send packages or money to consult the prison's specific rules or contact local authorities to confirm the acceptable items and processes, ensuring compliance with Brazilian regulations.[50] If you're unsure, consulting with a local lawyer specializing in criminal law or prison matters can provide guidance on how to proceed legally.

Mail and Visitation

Sending letters and visiting inmates in Brazilian prisons involve specific procedures and regulations that vary by facility. Letters to inmates can generally be sent without restrictions on quantity, but their contents will be reviewed by prison staff for security reasons. The inmate

---

48   https://oliveiralawyers.com/services/real-estate/acquisition/send-money-brazil/

49   https://www.bop.gov/inmates/communications.jsp#:~:text=Sending%20Packages

50   https://www.usa.gov/visit-prisoner-send-money

is responsible for purchasing postage for outgoing mail, and letters may be rejected if they contain prohibited content or are written in a foreign language, though consular assistance can be sought in such cases.

Visitation rights are governed by the Brazilian Penal Code and individual prison rules. Inmates have the right to receive visits from family, legal representatives, and approved individuals, but visits must be scheduled in advance. Visitors typically need to register on the prison's visitor list and undergo background checks and security screenings. The nature of the visit depends on the prison's security level and regulations, which could involve physical contact restrictions, limited visiting time (usually 30 minutes to an hour), and designated visiting areas. Visitors should always verify specific procedures, including allowed items and dress code, with the prison before visiting.

Both the letter-sending and visitation processes are designed to maintain security while allowing inmates to maintain connections with family and support networks. Rules can vary significantly between facilities, so checking with the specific prison is essential to avoid issues.

Prisoner Outreach

Prisoner outreach programs in Brazil have emerged as essential components in addressing the systemic issues faced by the country's overcrowded and underfunded penal system. These initiatives seek to rehabilitate inmates and reduce recidivism through various means, including educational opportunities, vocational training, and psychological support. For instance, the Association for the *Protection and Assistance of the Condemned* (APAC) employs a unique rehabilitative model that emphasizes dignity, love, and responsibility without relying on guards, instead empowering inmates to manage their facilities. This approach has been credited with significantly lowering recidivism rates to between 3 and 15 percent, compared to the traditional prison system, where the rates soar as high as 58 percent in São Paulo state.[51]

---

51 https://pfi.org/resources/stories-of-hope/apac-is-changing-lives-in-brazil/

Further enhancing rehabilitation efforts, the *Peace Education Program*, run by the *Prison Education Foundation* (FUNAP) in collaboration with The *Prem Rawat Foundation*, aims to instill personal peace and inner strength among inmates. This program has transformed the lives of numerous participants, helping them develop skills for reintegration into society and cultivate a sense of hope and purpose. The combination of these outreach initiatives not only aids individual inmates but also benefits communities by reducing crime and fostering safer environments.

Prison Scams

Prison scams in Brazil typically involve fraudsters exploiting the vulnerability of inmates and their families. Common scams include fake legal agents promising to arrange bail or legal representation for a fee, false prison fundraisers claiming to support inmates' basic needs, and impersonators who pose as inmates in danger to ask for money. There are also scams involving prison transfers, where criminals claim they can secure a transfer to a better facility for a fee, and scams around sending gifts or packages, where individuals ask for payment upfront. Additionally, scammers sometimes use phone calls or social media to deceive families by pretending to be an inmate or a prison official.

To avoid falling victim to these scams, it's crucial to verify any claims directly with the prison or through legitimate legal channels, use official methods for sending money or supplies, and be cautious of unsolicited requests. Always take time to assess situations carefully and consult professionals when in doubt.

Inmate Transfers to the United States[52]

Inmate transfers from Brazil to the United States occur under specific treaties and legal frameworks designed to facilitate the repatriation of foreign nationals. The U.S. and Brazil have established bilateral

---

52 https://br.usembassy.gov/u-s-citizen-services/
   assistance-u-s-citizens-arrested-brazil/

agreements that allow for the transfer of prisoners who are U.S. citizens serving sentences in Brazilian jails and wish to serve the remainder of their sentences back in the U.S. This process involves a thorough examination of the inmate's case, including considerations such as their willingness to transfer, the nature of their crimes, and their eligibility under U.S. laws.[53] Key requirements for the transfer include that the sentenced offense must also constitute a crime in the United States, which is known as "dual criminality," and both countries must consent to the transfer.

The transfer process is facilitated by the *International Prisoner Transfer Unit* (IPTU) within the U.S. Department of Justice, which coordinates with Brazilian authorities to ensure compliance with the relevant treaties. Upon acceptance of the transfer application, a *Consent Verification Hearing* (CVH) is conducted, where the inmate confirms their desire to return to the U.S. Following a successful CVH, Brazilian prison officials will arrange for the logistics of the transfer, including security measures and transportation to the U.S. This repatriation not only allows inmates to be closer to family support systems but also aims to facilitate their eventual reintegration into society upon release in the United States.

For more information, contact the American Citizen Services Section at the U.S. Embassy, or visit the U.S. Department of Justice's website for DOJ's International Prisoner Transfer Program at **http://www.justice.gov/ criminal/oeo/iptu/**.

Takeaways

1. It's important to consult with legal experts familiar with Brazilian criminal law and connect with your home country's embassy for guidance and assistance.

---

53 https://fam.state.gov/fam/07fam/07fam0480.html

2. Regular communication through mail, phone calls, and visits is vital for the emotional well-being of inmates. However, correspondence and visitation are subject to strict regulations, such as security checks and content reviews. Ensuring compliance with each prison's rules is key to maintaining these connections.

3. While it's possible to send financial support and care packages to inmates, strict regulations govern these practices.

4. Beware of prison scams! To avoid falling victim, always verify any claims through official channels such as the embassy or local legal authorities and use legitimate methods for sending money and supplies.

5. The process of transferring an inmate from Brazil to the U.S. is governed by bilateral agreements and requires the inmate's consent. Both countries must agree to the transfer, which is facilitated by the U.S. Department of Justice. Key criteria include "dual criminality," meaning the crime must be punishable in both countries.

CHAPTER 13

THE ADMINISTRATION
OF JUSTICE

CHAPTER 13

THE ADMINISTRATION
OF JUSTICE

Overview

The administration of justice consists of procedures for handling criminal or civil matters. It is known as criminal procedure (for criminal matters) or civil procedure (for civil or non-criminal matters).

The administration of justice is generally a formal, rule-based process that governs all aspects, including the right to bail when arrested in a criminal case, how evidence is presented in court, and who determines guilt or innocence (e.g., a judge or jury). It also dictates who decides the outcome of a civil case (e.g., a judge or jury).

Brazil's judiciary is a multifaceted system that operates on the state and federal levels, similar to the U.S. judicial system. Primarily based on the civil law tradition, Brazil divides cases into several different jurisdictions, including labor, electoral, military, constitutional, and non-constitutional. It also includes three instances of appeal, with cases able to advance from first-level courts all the way to either the Supreme Federal Court or the Superior Court of Justice. [54]

---

54 https://www.wilsoncenter.org/publication/the-brazilian-judicial-system

Brazil's Legal System

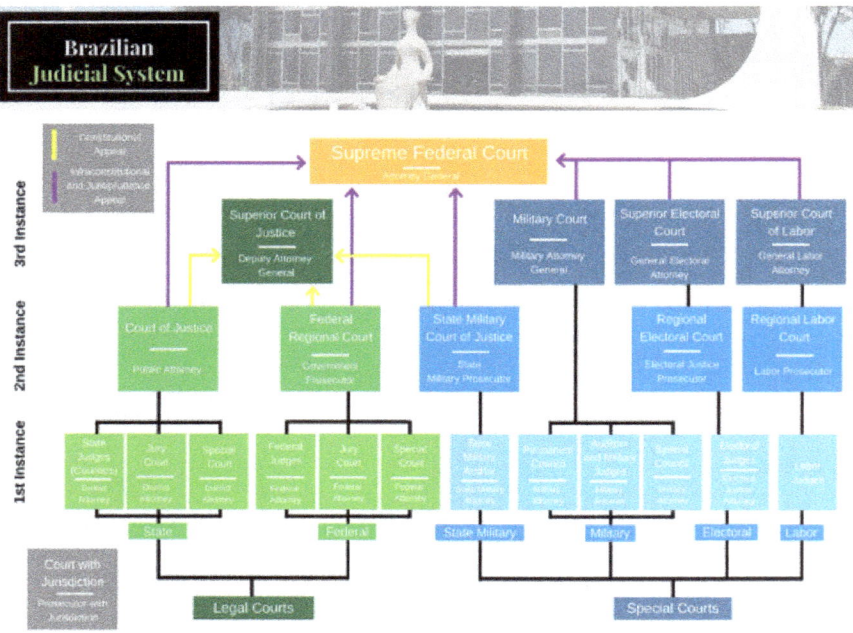

Brazil's legal system is a complex framework rooted in the civil law tradition, heavily influenced by Roman law and established during the Portuguese colonial period. The country operates under a federal constitution, which was enacted in 1988, characterizing Brazil as a federative republic consisting of 26 states and one federal district.[55] The Brazilian legal system is primarily codified, relying on statutes and regulations enacted by federal, state, and municipal legislatures, and is administered through a hierarchical court system. This system includes various levels of courts:

- **Supreme Court** (**STF**): The highest court in Brazil, responsible for safeguarding the Constitution and ruling on constitutional matters, as well as appeals on important legal issues.

---

55 https://maint.loc.gov/law/help/legal-research-guide/brazil-legal.php

- **Superior Court of Justice (STJ):** This court handles appeals in non-constitutional matters, ensuring uniformity in the interpretation of federal laws across the country.

- **Regional Federal Courts (TRFs):** These courts deal with cases involving federal law and have jurisdiction over specific geographic regions.

- **State Courts:** Each Brazilian state has its own court system, which includes courts of first instance, courts of appeal, and specialized courts (such as labor and electoral courts) that handle specific types of cases.

The Brazilian judiciary functions independently from the executive and legislative branches, ensuring a system of checks and balances crucial to the integrity of the rule of law.[56] Brazilian judges are appointed through rigorous examinations and must meet specific requirements, such as having a certain level of legal practice experience. Although Brazil does not strictly follow the doctrine of stare decisis (a legal doctrine that requires courts to follow previous judicial decisions in similar cases), as prevalent in common law systems, recent reforms have introduced a binding precedent mechanism that allows higher courts' decisions to guide lower courts on similar legal issues. Despite these advancements, challenges remain, including issues of overcrowding in prisons, access to justice, and systemic corruption within the legal framework.

---

56 https://judiciariesworldwide.fjc.gov/country-profile/brazil

LAW OF THE LAND BRAZIL

? General Questions

1. *Will the court treat first-time offenders and tourists with more leniency?* **No**. The Brazilian court system does not generally treat tourists with more leniency compared to local citizens. While some may perceive a degree of leniency in certain cases, tourists are subject to the same laws and legal processes as Brazilian nationals. Any violations of Brazilian law, such as drug offenses or public misconduct, can result in serious legal consequences, including detention and deportation, without preferential treatment.

2. *If I am charged with a crime, which court is likely to hear my case?* If a foreign national is charged with a crime while traveling in Brazil, the jurisdiction that will hear the case depends on the crime's nature and severity. Common crimes such as theft, assault, or drug offenses are typically heard in the state courts, specifically the first instance state courts (*Juízes de Primeiro Grau*) handle most criminal cases at the local level. In contrast, serious offenses like drug trafficking that involve federal jurisdiction will be overseen by the Federal Judiciary, which includes federal first instance courts (*Juízes Federais*) and Federal Regional Tribunals (*Tribunais Regionais Federais*). If the case raises constitutional questions, the Federal Supreme Court (Supremo Tribunal Federal) may also become involved as it addresses these specific legal issues.

3. *What is the standard of proof in a criminal case in Brazil?* In Brazil, criminal cases follow the "beyond a reasonable doubt" standard, as stated in Article 5, XXXIX of the Brazilian Constitution, which ensures no one is considered guilty until a final, unappealable conviction. The prosecution must present strong, reliable evidence to prove guilt, while the accused is entitled to a proper defense, including the right to confront witnesses and present counter-evidence. These safeguards uphold the presumption of innocence and require a solid case from the prosecution.

CRIME VICTIM ASSISTANCE

IN THIS CHAPTER

- Victim's Rights and Resources
- What to Do If You Are a Victim of a Crime
- American Citizen Services Unit
- Common Financial Scams and Crimes Affecting Visitors
- Tips for Avoiding Scams
- General Questions

CRIME VICTIM ASSISTANCE

Disclaimer: While this information is primarily intended for U.S. citizens, it can also serve as a general guideline for citizens of other countries. For more details specific to U.S. citizens, visit **https://br.usembassy.gov/u-s-citizen-services/victims-of-crime/**.

Victim's Rights and Resources[57]

Brazilian law recognizes the rights of crime victims and offers various resources to support individuals affected by crime. This legal framework seeks to ensure that victims receive the necessary assistance, protection, and recognition within the criminal justice system. The Constitution of Brazil, particularly in Article 5, provides for the dignity, legal protection, and assistance of victims, emphasizing their rights to compensation and to participate in legal proceedings. The rights of crime victims, however, are often multifaceted and can vary depending on the nature of the crime and the legal context.

---

57 https://travel.state.gov/content/travel/en/international-travel/emergencies/crime.html#ExternalPopup

Legal Rights of Crime Victims[58]

In Brazil, victims have a right to receive information about the criminal process and protection measures throughout legal proceedings. Brazilian law mandates that victims are entitled to measures that ensure their safety, particularly in cases of domestic violence, sexual assault, and human trafficking (Human Rights in Brazil - Amnesty International). For instance, the *Maria da Penha Law*, implemented to combat domestic violence, stipulates protective measures that can be put in place to ensure the safety of victims, allowing them to receive necessary support through legal and social services Additionally, victims can participate in legal proceedings as a part of the prosecution, which allows them to present evidence and give testimony, reinforcing their role in the justice process.

Moreover, the legal system provides avenues for compensation, where victims may seek reparation for damages through civil actions. The Brazilian government also recognizes the need for psychological support, treatment, and ancillary services specifically designed to assist victims in coping with the aftermath of crime. These rights and resources reflect Brazil's commitment to providing comprehensive support for crime victims, enhancing their ability to recover and participate in the justice system.

Resources Available for Crime Victims

To facilitate access to justice and support for crime victims, Brazil has established several organizations and resources. The *Women's Call Center* (**Call 180**) is a notable example that provides a channel for women experiencing violence to receive immediate assistance, guidance, and information regarding their rights and available services. Various non-governmental organizations (NGOs) also play a crucial role in advocating for victims' rights. For example, organizations like the *Instituto Maria da Penha* work to empower women and promote awareness regarding

---

58 https://resourcehub.bakermckenzie.com/en/resources/fighting-domestic-violence/latin-america-and-the-caribbean/brazil/topics/1legal-provisions

domestic violence laws, providing educational resources and community support initiatives.

Local police stations often have dedicated units that cater to the needs of crime victims, offering counseling, legal advice, and assistance in navigating the reporting process. Furthermore, the Brazilian government has initiated programs to better coordinate victim support services across social, health, and legal sectors.[59] These resources are vital in helping victims understand their rights, access necessary services, and heal from the trauma of criminal acts.

What to Do if You Are a Victim of a Crime

If you are a foreign national who becomes a victim of a crime in Brazil, here are the key steps to follow:

1. **Ensure Your Safety:** First and foremost, ensure your immediate safety. If you are in danger or need urgent medical attention, contact emergency services by calling **190** (police) or **192** (ambulance) in Brazil.

2. **Report the Crime to the Police:** You should report the crime to the local police (*Delegacia*). Many police stations have specific units for foreign nationals or tourist areas, and you may find someone who speaks English. Be sure to provide detailed information about the incident.

3. **Contact Your Embassy or Consulate:** Inform your home country's embassy or consulate in Brazil as soon as possible. They can offer support, provide legal assistance, help with language barriers, and sometimes assist with communication with the police. The embassy may also help you contact a lawyer or translator if needed.

4. **File a Police Report (Boletim de Ocorrência):** A police report, known as a *Boletim de Ocorrência*, is required for legal proceedings

---

59 https://www.ictj.org/location/brazil

and insurance claims. The police will provide you with a copy of this report. Be aware that in Brazil, it is mandatory to report all crimes.

5. **Seek Legal Assistance:** Consider seeking legal advice, particularly if you are involved in a legal process. Many embassies provide lists of English-speaking lawyers who specialize in criminal law. Some NGOs also offer legal support for victims of crime.

6. **Document Everything:** Keep a record of all communications, reports, and any evidence related to the crime. Take photos of injuries, property damage, or other relevant details, as these may be important for police investigations or insurance claims.

7. **Contact Your Insurance Provider:** If the crime involves theft or property damage, contact your travel or health insurance provider. They may assist in covering medical costs, lost property, or other related expenses.

If the crime involves an assault or medical emergency, Brazil's public health system (SUS) may offer medical care, often at little or no cost. Additionally, consider contacting victim support services in Brazil, as several NGOs and organizations provide psychological counseling, particularly for those who have experienced violent crime or traumatic events. It's also important to stay in contact with the authorities to track the progress of the investigation. While the process may take time, you will want to keep updated on all developments.

American Citizen Services Unit

American Citizen Services (ACS) in Brazil is another important resource for American visitors. The ACS Unit is part of the U.S. Embassy or Consulate, providing essential services to U.S. citizens living or traveling abroad. Its primary functions include:

- **Emergency Assistance:** Helping Americans in distress, such as those who are victims of crime, hospitalized, or involved in accidents.

- **Consular Services:** Providing passport renewals, reports of birth abroad, and other vital documents.

- **Legal and Financial Assistance:** Offering guidance on legal issues, such as arrest or detention, and providing information on local legal resources or attorneys.

- **Travel Advisories and Safety Information:** Keeping citizens informed about safety issues and travel alerts in the host country.

- **Assistance with Family Emergencies:** Helping with cases of missing persons, death, or other urgent family matters.

The ACS unit acts as a bridge between U.S. citizens and local authorities, offering critical support and ensuring that Americans receive their rights and protections while abroad. For more information or to request services, U.S. citizens can contact the U.S. Embassy in Brasília or the nearest consulate in cities such as São Paulo, Rio de Janeiro, or Recife.

Common Financial Scams and Crimes Affecting Visitors

Brazil, while known for its vibrant culture and stunning landscapes, is also a country where visitors need to be cautious of various financial scams and crimes. Tourists are often seen as easier targets due to their unfamiliarity with local customs and legal systems, making them vulnerable to a range of deceptive practices. Some of the most prevalent scams include currency exchange fraud, pickpocketing, and online scams, particularly those linked to social media and dating platforms.

One of the most common scams involves currency exchange, where tourists are deceived into accepting counterfeit bills or unfavorable exchange rates from unscrupulous street vendors or kiosks. Additionally, pickpocketing is a frequent occurrence, particularly in crowded tourist hotspots and public transportation. Skilled criminals often work in teams, creating distractions to divert the victim's attention while another thief stealthily steals wallets, phones, or other valuables, highlighting the importance of vigilance in busy areas.

Online scams also pose a significant threat, with criminals exploiting digital platforms to perpetrate romance scams or fake rental listings.

Tourists may receive unsolicited messages on social media from individuals posing as locals who feign friendship or romance before requesting financial assistance for various spurious reasons. The rise of dating apps has further exacerbated this issue, as unsuspecting individuals can find themselves entangled in scams that initially seem genuine but ultimately lead to financial loss.

Also common are fake tour guides and taxi scams that involve unlicensed individuals charging inflated rates or taking longer routes. To avoid this, always use licensed taxis or reputable ride-sharing apps and book tours through trusted agencies. Overcharging is common in tourist areas, with businesses inflating prices for goods and services; always confirm prices and ask for receipts. Fake police officers may demand identification and bribes; insist on seeing proper ID and contact the real police if in doubt. "Fake" emergency scams involve scammers claiming that friends or family are in urgent need of money; verify such stories before sending funds. Credit card fraud occurs through methods like phishing or skimming; monitor transactions and use secure payment methods. Hotel and accommodation scams include false booking websites or substandard accommodations; always book through reputable sites. Finally, fake fundraising scams involve individuals posing as charity workers; verify the legitimacy of such organizations before donating.

In addition to financial scams, more serious offenses such as theft, robbery, and even violent crime can impact tourists in Brazil. Areas with high tourist traffic, like Rio de Janeiro and São Paulo, have reported incidents of armed robberies targeting visitors, especially at night. Tourists are encouraged to remain aware of their surroundings, avoid displaying wealth, and opt for reputable transportation services to mitigate the risk of such crimes. Increased awareness and understanding of the landscape of scams and crimes in Brazil can significantly enhance a visitor's safety and overall experience while exploring this beautiful country.

Tips for Avoiding Scams

- **Be cautious with personal information:** Don't share your financial or personal details with strangers.

- **Use reputable services:** Book taxis, tours, and accommodation through trusted and verified platforms.

- **Secure your belongings:** Keep your valuables in a secure place, such as a hotel safe, and use anti-theft bags.

- **Verify emergency situations:** Always confirm urgent requests through official channels, whether it's about medical emergencies or legal issues.

- **Report fraud:** If you are a victim of fraud, report it to local authorities and your embassy.

General Questions

1. *If I am the victim of a crime, can I legally be compensated?*
   Yes. If you're a victim of a crime in Brazil, you may be eligible for compensation, depending on the crime and circumstances. Victims of violent crimes may receive compensation through criminal proceedings, where the court may order the offender to pay damages. Civil lawsuits can also be filed for financial losses or suffering. Brazil offers public compensation for victims of violent crimes through the Crime Victim Assistance Fund, which can help cover medical expenses or funeral costs. Additionally, if you have insurance, you may be able to claim for medical or property losses. However, seeking compensation can be challenging, especially if the perpetrator is not caught or lacks financial resources.

2. *As a tourist, who should I contact for assistance if I am the victim of a crime?* After contacting the proper authorities, you should contact your home country's embassy or consulate that can provide assistance to crime victims by offering guidance on local laws, helping connect with legal representation, facilitating communication with family, and supporting the victim through the legal process. They can also assist in obtaining necessary documents and provide emergency support, such as arranging for medical care or repatriation.

POLICE

POLICE

Overview

As of 2022, the total number of police officers in Brazil is approximately 464,600, which includes federal, state, and municipal law enforcement personnel. This workforce is part of a broader public administration sector that employs about 8.1 million individuals across various governmental roles.[60] The size of the police force is critical in addressing crime and maintaining public safety in a country facing significant security challenges.

The staffing of the police force in Brazil is often considered inadequate, as evidenced by a significant disparity between police personnel and the country's large population, which exceeds 210 million. Reports indicate that many regions struggle with insufficient police officer numbers to effectively respond to crime and maintain public safety. Moreover, issues such as high turnover rates, training deficiencies, and poor working conditions contribute to challenges in adequately staffing police forces across the nation, affecting overall effectiveness in combating crime and ensuring security.[61]

---

60 https://www.statista.com/statistics/763742/
    number-employees-public-administration-sector-brazil

61 https://www.redalyc.org/journal/2734/273476409010/html

The Brazilian police face a myriad of challenges, notably the pervasive issues of corruption, systemic violence, and a high rate of killings resulting from police operations. Corruption is rampant, with many officers implicated in organized crime and extortion, undermining public trust and efficacy.[62] Furthermore, police brutality is a significant concern, as evidenced by high homicide rates attributed to law enforcement, with over 6,000 annual killings reported.[63] Calls for reform are urgent, emphasizing the need for improved training, accountability, and a shift toward community policing methods to foster trust and reduce lethal encounters). Additionally, socio-political factors, such as the support for militarized policing strategies, complicate efforts to implement effective and humane security measures.[64]

Brazilian Law Enforcement[65]

The Brazilian police system is structured into several distinct entities, categorized by federal, state, and municipal levels, each with specific responsibilities defined by the Federal Constitution.

At the federal level, there are four primary institutions: the Federal Police (*Polícia Federal*), the Federal Highway Police (*Polícia Rodoviária Federal*), the Federal Railway Police (*Polícia Ferroviária Federal*), and the Federal Penal Police (*Polícia Penal Federal*). These were established to address crimes that affect federal interests, such as drug trafficking and terrorism. The Federal Police primarily investigates national crimes and provides support in integrating police forces across Brazil.

---

62   https://insightcrime.org/news/
     brazil-ceara-large-scale-criminal-networks-police/

63   https://www.hrw.org/news/2024/10/10/
     un-experts-spotlight-devastating-police-brutality-brazil

64   https://valorinternational.globo.com/economy/news/2023/08/14/bra-
     zils-ministry-of-justice-working-to-update-police-training.ghtml

65   https://oliveiralawyers.com/about-brazil/brazil-legal/criminal-system/
     law-enforcement-brazil/

At the state level, the military police (*Polícia Militar*) is tasked with maintaining public order and performing preventive patrols, while the civil police (*Polícia Civil*) conducts investigations of criminal offenses. These agencies operate under the jurisdiction of the state governors and are crucial in law enforcement within their respective states.

Municipal Guards (*Guardas Municipais*) at the municipal level serve as auxiliary police forces, focusing on safeguarding local properties and public spaces while supporting other law enforcement agencies in criminal matters. Although they are primarily responsible for protecting municipal assets, their roles have been evolving to encompass community safety and rights protection, especially in densely populated urban areas.

Each level of police force plays a crucial role in Brazil's broader justice system, responding to different layers of criminal activity while facing challenges such as corruption, public distrust, and violent crime. The collaboration among federal, state, and municipal forces is essential for ensuring effective law enforcement and community safety across the diverse landscapes of Brazil.

Police and Community Relations[66]

The image and reputation of the Brazilian police are marred by deep-seated issues that undermine public trust and confidence. According to various surveys, over 60 percent of Brazilians express dissatisfaction with police performance, attributing their discontent to a long history of corruption, extrajudicial killings, and the use of excessive force.[67] For instance, a notable study revealed that 63 percent of respondents reported being unsatisfied with police effectiveness, with the armed forces often viewed more favorably as a trusted security institution. This troubling perception is compounded by rampant cases of police brutality, where

---

66 https://www.statista.com/statistics/1453089/trust-in-the-police-force-in-brazil/#:~:text=In%20July%202024%2C%2070%20percent,share%20this%20feeling%20of%20trust

67 https://insightcrime.org/news/brief/over-60-of-brazilians-distrust-the-police-survey/

officers are implicated in thousands of deaths annually, particularly targeting marginalized communities. The notion that police are seen as an enemy rather than protector is prevalent in many impoverished areas, illustrating a significant barrier to community safety and cooperation.[68]

Moreover, police violence and corruption have contributed to a pervasive climate of fear among the population, forcing many to view law enforcement as a greater threat than criminal organizations themselves. Black Brazilians, in particular, report a heightened fear of police violence, with statistics showing that they are disproportionately affected by state violence remains one of mistrust and skepticism, necessitating comprehensive reforms to restore public confidence and foster a more positive image.[69]

Police Use of Force

Excessive force and police brutality are significant issues in Brazil due to poor working conditions, low pay, and inadequate training, particularly in community policing and de-escalation tactics. The result is widespread corruption, violence, and a lack of accountability. Each year, Brazilian police kill over 6,000 people, with people of African descent disproportionately affected. Impunity for police misconduct, along with a lack of trust both within the police force and the local communities, exacerbates the problem. There are also reports of extrajudicial executions and high-profile massacres in cities like São Paulo and Rio de Janeiro. In response, several investigative commissions have called for reforms, including demilitarizing the police, implementing independent oversight, introducing less-lethal weapons, mandating body cameras, and ensuring that police investigations are free from internal interference. These reforms are critical to restoring public trust and improving the effectiveness of law enforcement in Brazil. Without such changes,

---

68 https://www.statista.com/topics/7861/police-vio-lence-in-brazil/#:~:text=The%20curse%20of%20racial%20profiling

69 https://www1.folha.uol.com.br/internacional/en/brazil/2024/12/brazil-ians-fear-the-police-more-than-they-trust-it-says-datafolha.shtml

public mistrust will continue to undermine the police force's ability to ensure safety and justice.

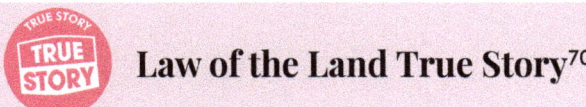

Law of the Land True Story[70]

Outrage In São Paulo Over Police Brutality. A disturbing video of a São Paulo state police officer pushing an unarmed man off an overpass has sparked outrage and highlighted the rise in police violence under Governor Tarcísio de Freitas. The footage shows the victim, a motorcycle delivery driver, being thrown into a sewage-filled stream. The officer was arrested, and 12 others were suspended. This incident is part of a broader trend of rising police killings since Freitas, a former Jair Bolsonaro ally, took office in 2023. Despite claims of "moderation," Freitas has been criticized for fostering a culture of police repression, with officers feeling emboldened to use lethal force. Sociologists argue that this violence disproportionately impacts poor and Black communities, particularly in marginalized São Paulo neighborhoods. Freitas' defense of the police and dismissal of human rights concerns have led to growing calls for accountability, with critics accusing him of using this violence to consolidate far-right support.

---

70 https://www.theguardian.com/world/2024/dec/05/
   sao-paulo-police-violence

CHAPTER 16

HOW TO GET LEGAL HELP IN BRAZIL

HOW TO GET LEGAL HELP IN BRAZIL

Available Resources

If you find yourself arrested in Brazil, the Constitution provides you with several fundamental rights to ensure your protection and fair treatment:

- **Right to Be Informed:** You must be informed of the reasons for your arrest.
- **Right to Legal Counsel:** You have the right to access legal representation, including free legal assistance if you cannot afford a lawyer.
- **Right to Judicial Review:** Your detention must be reviewed by a judge, who will assess the legality of your arrest.
- **Protection from Arbitrary Arrest:** Arrests must be based on a judicial warrant, except when caught in the act of committing a crime.
- **Right to Be Informed of Rights:** You should be informed of your rights at the time of your arrest.
- **Right to Remain Silent:** You have the right to remain silent to avoid self-incrimination during questioning by law enforcement.

Legal Aid

In Brazil, foreigners have the same legal rights as Brazilian citizens. Brazilian law ensures that anyone who cannot afford legal representation is entitled to free legal aid. The Public Defender's Office (*Defensoria Pública*) provides free legal counsel and support to individuals unable to cover the cost of legal proceedings which extends to foreigners, including asylum seekers, refugees, and those facing legal issues in the country.

The Defensoria Pública operates throughout Brazil, across all states and major cities, and is divided into two main branches: the State Public Defender's Office (*Defensoria Pública do Estado*) and the Federal Public Defender's Office (*Defensoria Pública da União*), based on the type of case.

- **Federal Public Defender's Office:** Handles cases related to asylum, social welfare, foreigners' rights, and criminal proceedings before federal courts (e.g., cases involving forged documents, deportation, or extradition).
- **State Public Defender's Office:** Deals with civil matters like housing, custody, and divorce, as well as criminal cases in state courts (e.g., homicide, fraud, embezzlement, sexual offenses).

Foreign nationals can access legal aid by visiting the local Defensoria Pública office or reaching out to them for assistance in cases of criminal charges, immigration issues, or other legal concerns. The Defensoria Pública da União provides specialized assistance for matters such as asylum and refugee rights.

You can find more detailed contact information on the Defensoria Pública website at **https://www.dpu.def.br/contatos-dpu**, where you can locate regional offices and learn more about services available in your area. However, bear in mind the site is in Portuguese, so you may need a translation tool to navigate it.

Foreign Embassies in Brazil

Brazil is home to numerous foreign embassies that represent the interests of their respective countries. These embassies offer a range of services to their citizens, such as consular support, emergency assistance, visa issuance, and legal guidance. The capital, Brasília, is the location of 131 embassies, while the country also hosts 536 consulates and three other diplomatic missions.

Foreign embassies and consulates in Brazil are primarily concentrated in major cities. Brasília, the capital, hosts most embassies due to its role as the political and diplomatic center of the country. São Paulo, the largest city and economic hub, is home to numerous consulates, serving both business and tourist populations. Rio de Janeiro, a cultural and tourist center, also has several consulates. Other cities like Porto Alegre, Recife, and Manaus have consular offices, mainly for regional trade, business, and diplomatic purposes. These locations are chosen for their economic, cultural, or political significance in Brazil.

List of U.S. Embassies and Consulates in Brazil

U.S. Embassy Brasília

SES, Av. das Nações, Quadra 801, Lote 03
70403-900 - Brasília, DF
Phone: 55 (61) 3312-7687
Fax: 55 (61) 3323-1972
E-mail: imprensabrasilia@state.gov

U.S. Consulate General Rio de Janeiro

Av. Presidente Wilson, 147 – Centro
20030-020 – Rio de Janeiro, RJ
Phone: 55 (21) 3823-2169 / 55 21 3823-2119
Fax: 55 (21) 3823-2121 / 2122
E-mail: imprensario@state.gov

U.S. Consulate General São Paulo

Rua Henri Dunant, 500, Chácara Santo Antônio

04709-110 – São Paulo- SP

Phone: 55 (11) 5186-5237

Fax: 55 (11) 5181-1368

E-mail: imprensasp@state.gov

U.S. Consulate Recife

Rua Gonçalves Maia, 163 Boa Vista

50070-060 - Recife, PE

Phone: 55 (81) 3416-3063

Fax: 55 (81) 3231-1906

E-mail: imprensarecife@state.gov

 For a list of other foreign embassies and consulates in Brazil, please visit **https://embassies.net/brazil.**

 **Law of the Land Hypothetical**

HYPOTHETICAL: *Raul, a foreign national, is arrested in Brazil on charges of theft. He is unable to afford a private attorney and, as per Brazilian law, he is entitled to a public defender. However, Raul quickly realizes that his assigned public defender seems overworked, with a heavy caseload, and lacks the resources to effectively challenge the evidence against him. The defender barely meets with him, and Raul feels his defense is not being taken seriously. In addition, Raul's case is complicated by the fact that he does not speak Portuguese fluently, making communication with his public defender even more difficult. Raul wonders if there is anything he can do to ensure he gets competent legal representation.*

What should Raul do if he feels that his public defender is not providing him with competent legal representation, and what steps can he take to address this issue?

ANSWER: *In Brazil, public defenders are required to represent those who cannot afford a private lawyer, but their effectiveness can vary by location. In larger cities, they generally have more resources, while rural areas may face shortages. If Raul feels his public defender is not providing adequate representation, he should contact his embassy. The embassy can intervene by ensuring Raul receives proper legal support, helping with communication, or even facilitating a change of public defender. They may also provide a list of English-speaking attorneys if needed. The embassy's assistance can help ensure Raul's legal rights are protected.*

MEDICAL FACILITIES & HOSPITALS

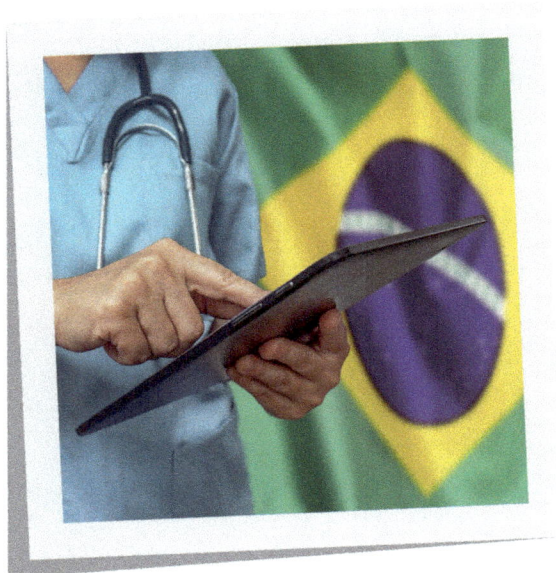

MEDICAL FACILITIES & HOSPITALS

Overview[71]

Brazil's healthcare system is a dual structure that combines a universal public system with a robust private sector. The public healthcare system, known as *Sistema Único de Saúde* (SUS), provides free medical services to all residents, including emergency care for tourists, regardless of their nationality. The SUS system aims to offer comprehensive coverage, ranging from preventive care to hospital services, but it faces challenges such as underfunding, overcrowding, and long wait times, particularly in rural areas. Despite these issues, SUS plays a crucial role in providing healthcare access to Brazil's large population.

The private healthcare sector in Brazil is well-developed and caters to those who can afford insurance or out-of-pocket payments. Private hospitals and clinics are known for their high standards of care, advanced medical technology, and specialization in areas such as cosmetic surgery, fertility treatments, and dermatology. Many private hospitals in urban centers are equipped with internationally trained staff, and the country is a popular destination for medical tourism, particularly for cosmetic and elective procedures. However, the private sector is only accessible to a small proportion of the population, as the cost can be prohibitive.

---

71 https://www.internationalinsurance.com/hospitals/brazil/

Visitors' Access to Healthcare in Brazil

Visitors to Brazil can access medical services, but the coverage and conditions depend on the type of care they need. The SUS, Brazil's public healthcare system, provides emergency medical care to all individuals, including tourists, free of charge. This service is available in case of genuine emergencies, such as accidents or sudden illnesses, but does not cover pre-existing conditions or non-emergency situations like routine check-ups or elective procedures.

For non-emergency medical needs, tourists are generally advised to rely on private healthcare services. Brazil has a well-developed private healthcare sector, especially in urban areas and tourist destinations, with many hospitals and clinics offering high-quality care. However, these services typically require payment upfront or through private health insurance. Visitors are strongly encouraged to have travel insurance that includes medical coverage, as this can help cover the costs of private healthcare. Private hospitals may also ask for a significant deposit upon admission, with the option to apply for reimbursement through the visitor's insurance provider.[72]

Insurance Guidance

When traveling to Brazil, understanding the validity of foreign insurance plans is essential for ensuring access to high-quality medical care. While the SUS allows all individuals, including undocumented foreigners, to receive medical attention, foreign insurance plans may not be universally accepted at all healthcare facilities, especially those in the public sector. As a result, travelers are often recommended to maintain their private health insurance plans from their home countries to cover costs incurred at private hospitals and clinics, which typically offer a higher standard of care and shorter waiting times.

Moreover, it is prudent for travelers to confirm whether their insurance provider offers international coverage that explicitly includes Brazil.

---

72 https://www.internationalinsurance.com/health/systems/brazil.php

Some insurers may have partnerships with Brazilian healthcare providers, allowing for better access and facilitation of payments. Foreign travelers should also carry documentation detailing their insurance coverage, including the policy number and contact information for their insurance provider, to streamline access to necessary medical services during their stay. Ultimately, while foreign insurance plans may not be accepted universally within Brazil's public healthcare framework, they can be invaluable for navigating private medical care, ensuring travelers are adequately protected against unexpected health expenses during their visit.

Also keep in mind that the private hospitals and clinics that accept foreign insurance, may not have a direct billing agreement with your insurance provider. In such a case, you will likely need to pay for medical services upfront and then submit a claim for reimbursement. Keep all receipts and medical documents to submit for reimbursement once you return home or as required by your insurance company.

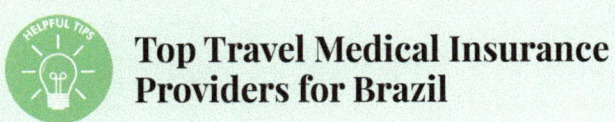

Top Travel Medical Insurance Providers for Brazil

1. **World Nomads:** Popular among travelers for flexible policies and coverage for adventure activities.

2. **Allianz Global Assistance:** Offers comprehensive travel insurance, including medical coverage for various needs.

3. **Travel Guard:** Provides a variety of plans with medical coverage tailored for travelers.

4. **IMG (International Medical Group):** Offers different travel medical insurance options to suit a range of traveler needs.

Brazil's Hospitals

As of 2022, Brazil has a total of 7,191 hospitals operating across the country.[73] In terms of medical staff, according to the most recent statistics Brazil has close to half a million registered physicians, translating to about 2.18 physicians per 1,000 inhabitants.[74]

While there is a notable quantity of healthcare resources, their distribution and effectiveness in providing comprehensive care remain significant challenges for Brazil with significant regional disparities, particularly between urban and rural areas. Many rural regions are inadequately served, while urban centers are often oversaturated with healthcare resources. In Brazil, hospitals are primarily concentrated in large urban centers and major cities, with São Paulo, Rio de Janeiro, Brasília, Belo Horizonte, and Salvador being home to many high-quality medical facilities, particularly private hospitals. These cities offer a wide range of specialized care and cater to both local and international patients. Additionally, tourist hotspots like Florianópolis, Porto Alegre, Fortaleza, and Recife also have well-developed healthcare infrastructures to support medical tourism.

Hospitals for International Visitors

Brazil is increasingly recognized as a major destination for medical tourism, attracting international patients for a wide range of medical treatments, particularly in areas such as cosmetic surgery, dental care, fertility treatments, orthopedics, and cardiovascular care. The country offers high-quality healthcare at competitive prices, making it an attractive option for international patients. Major cities like São Paulo, Rio de Janeiro, and Belo Horizonte host top-tier hospitals that cater to foreign patients, offering services such as multilingual support and concierge services. Several hospitals in Brazil cater specifically to international visitors, offering services in English, accepting international insurance, and providing high-quality medical care. These hospitals are especially

---

73 https://www.statista.com/statistics/1070776/brazil-number-hospitals/

74 https://www.commonwealthfund.org/international-health-policy-center/countries/brazil

popular among tourists, expatriates, and medical tourists. Some of the most notable hospitals that cater to international visitors include:

- **Hospital Sírio-Libanês (São Paulo):** One of Brazil's most renowned private hospitals, Hospital Sírio-Libanês is known for its excellence in medical care and a strong focus on international patients. It offers a wide range of services, including emergency care, elective surgeries, and specialized treatments. The hospital has a dedicated international patient department, which helps coordinate medical care, language services, and insurance claims for foreign visitors.

- **Hospital Israelita Albert Einstein (São Paulo):** This is another leading private hospital in Brazil, well-regarded for treating both Brazilian citizens and international patients. It has a specialized international patient department that helps foreign visitors with logistics, from the initial consultation to post-treatment care. The hospital offers services in multiple languages, including English, and has strong international connections with insurers and medical providers worldwide.

- **Rede D'Or São Luiz (Multiple Locations):** Rede D'Or São Luiz is a large private healthcare network with hospitals across Brazil, including in major cities like São Paulo, Rio de Janeiro, and Brasília. Many of their hospitals cater to international patients, offering multilingual support and the ability to work directly with foreign insurance companies. Some of their facilities even have dedicated departments to assist international visitors, providing a seamless experience from admission to discharge.

- **Hospital de Câncer de Barretos (Private Wing, São Paulo):** Although primarily a public institution, Hospital de Câncer de Barretos also has a private wing that is renowned for its world-class cancer treatment services. It caters to international patients seeking advanced cancer care and offers assistance with travel arrangements, language services, and insurance claims. The hospital is equipped with the latest technology and has partnerships with international organizations, making it a top choice for medical tourism in oncology.

- **Clínica São Vicente (Rio de Janeiro):** Clínica São Vicente is a prominent private hospital in Rio de Janeiro that offers specialized care in a wide range of medical fields. The hospital has a reputation for serving international patients, offering multilingual support and assisting with logistics such as hospital transfers, visa assistance, and insurance coordination.

These hospitals are equipped to handle the needs of international visitors by offering multilingual support, international insurance partnerships, and specialized care. Many of them have dedicated departments to ensure a smooth experience for foreign patients, including help with travel logistics, translation services, and insurance processing.

 ## Cost of Medical Services

Typical medical costs in Brazil can vary widely based on the type of treatment and the region. Here are average costs for common treatments:

- **General consultation:** Around R$200 to R$400 (approximately US$40 to US$80).

- **Blood tests:** R$50 to R$150 (approximately US$10 to US$30).

- **X-rays:** R$100 to R$300 (approximately US$20 to US$60).

- **Minor surgeries:** R$1,000 to R$3,000 (approximately US$200 to US$600).

- **Major surgeries:** R$5,000 to R$20,000 (approximately US$1,000 to US$4,000), depending on complexity.

While medical costs are significantly lower in Brazil than in the United States, a medical emergency can still be a costly event for an average traveler, and you may want to consider purchasing travel medical insurance in case of unforeseen medical emergencies during your trip.

Medical Emergencies

What Should You Do If You Feel Unwell or Sick in Brazil?

If you experience a medical emergency in Brazil, act quickly to ensure you receive care.

For non-emergencies, visit a *Basic Health Unit (UBS)* for primary care, diagnosis, and treatment. For mild symptoms like a cold or flu, over-the-counter medications can provide temporary relief. Pharmacies are widespread, and pharmacists can offer advice. Monitor your symptoms and seek medical care for serious symptoms, like high fever or severe abdominal pain.

In an emergency, call **192** for an ambulance. This public service is available to everyone, including foreign visitors. Provide clear details about your location and emergency. Ambulances usually arrive promptly in cities, but response times may vary in rural areas. Paramedics will assess your condition and decide if transport to a hospital is necessary. Public services are free but may involve longer wait times, while private health insurance ensures quicker, personalized care. Have your insurance documents ready.

Keep records of your treatment for follow-up care or insurance claims. Lastly, inform your embassy or consulate, as they can provide assistance navigating the medical system. Being prepared can make a significant difference in managing a medical emergency in Brazil.

DRIVING IN BRAZIL

DRIVING IN BRAZIL[75]

Overview

Brazil is a huge country with a wide road network spanning more than 1.6 million kilometers (about 994,000 miles). The road conditions in Brazil can vary significantly depending on the region. In major cities and urban areas, the roads are generally well-maintained, with modern highways and infrastructure, though traffic congestion can be a challenge, especially in large cities like São Paulo and Rio de Janeiro. However, in rural areas and smaller towns, road conditions can be much more variable, with some roads poorly maintained, unpaved, or prone to flooding during the rainy season. While Brazil has an extensive network of highways (especially in the south and southeast), certain regions, such as the Amazon, still have isolated areas with limited access. In general, highways in the south and southeast tend to be in better condition than those in the north and northeast, where resources for road maintenance are more limited. Additionally, driving standards can be inconsistent, with aggressive driving and a lack of respect for traffic laws common in some areas. Travelers should be cautious and aware of local driving conditions and ensure their vehicles are equipped for the terrain, especially in more remote regions.

---

75 https://www.justlanded.com/english/Brazil/Brazil-Guide/Travel-Leisure/ Driving-in-Brazil

Required Documentation

Foreigners are allowed to drive in Brazil for up to 180 days after entering the country if they have a valid driver's license from their home country. During this period, you must carry your passport with you when you drive in addition to your license. If you intend to stay in Brazil more than 180 days, you will need to obtain a Brazilian driver's license. Foreigners can obtain a driver's license in Brazil through a simple process that may vary depending on their nationality and residency status.

 **Traffic Rules and Regulations**

Here are some important rules which apply to drivers anywhere in Brazil. Breaking any of the following rules would be considered a violation of the law:

- Be at least 18 years old to drive a car or motorcycle.

- Drive on the right, overtake on the left.

- Seatbelts must be worn by both drivers and passengers. In the case of a child that is too small to wear a seat belt, the child must have a specially fitted seatbelt.

- Mobile phones can only be used with a "hands-free" system.

- Do not run out of gas because it is illegal to do so.

- Do not drive wearing flip flops because it is also illegal (quirky law!).

- **Drinking and driving:** blood alcohol level of 0.02% or higher is considered illegal.

- Vehicles entering a roundabout must give way to the vehicles already on the roundabout.

- No right turns at red lights unless indicated through *Livre A Direita* signs.

- Basic third-party insurance is included in the road tax; the law does not require any additional insurance.

Be aware that pedestrian crossings are completely ignored in most places with only a few exceptions, such as in Brasilia. Stop signs would be better described as a yield sign and, virtually any lane could be a turning lane. Also, where there are sudden, unexpected traffic jams, drivers may wave their hands out the window or use emergency lights to signal other drivers to slow down.

Safety Recommendations

Driving in Brazil requires caution and preparation. Traffic can be congested, particularly in cities like São Paulo and Rio de Janeiro, and road conditions may vary, especially in rural areas. It's important to drive defensively, maintain a safe distance, and be aware of aggressive driving behaviors. Avoid driving at night in unfamiliar areas due to safety risks, and always wear seatbelts, as it's mandatory. Be mindful of pedestrians, motorcyclists, and potential car thefts in high-crime areas. Keep valuables out of sight and park in secure areas. Use GPS or navigation apps for direction and ensure your vehicle is in good condition for long trips. Lastly, be prepared for toll roads and carry extra fuel, water, and snacks for remote areas. Also, remember that many drivers in Brazil carry firearms for personal protection so avoid confrontations!

General Questions

1. *Can I use my driver's license from my home country to drive in Brazil?* **Yes**, you may use your driver's license in Brazil, but only up to 180 days.

2. *What is the legal minimum age to drive in Brazil?* In Brazil, you must be 18 to drive and operate a motor vehicle.

3. *What is the age requirement for renting a car in Brazil?* The minimum age requirement for renting a car is generally 21 years old. However, some rental agencies may have a minimum age of 25, particularly for larger or more expensive vehicles. Drivers under 25 may also be subject to a "young driver" surcharge. Additionally, renters must have held a valid driver's license for at least one year, and an international driving permit (IDP) may be required for non-residents.

NUDE BEACHES & CLOTHING-OPTIONAL RESORTS

NUDE BEACHES & CLOTHING-OPTIONAL RESORTS

Overview

While Brazil is not widely known for a mainstream nudist culture, it does have a well-established and growing community of naturism, particularly along its coastal areas. The country has a number of designated nudist beaches, resorts, and associations that cater to people seeking a clothing-free environment. Some of the most popular nudist beaches in Brazil include Praia do Pinho in Santa Catarina and Praia de Tambaba in Paraíba, both of which have long been favored by locals and international naturists.

Brazil's approach to nudism tends to be relaxed, particularly in more remote or private settings. However, public nudity outside designated areas is not generally accepted and can be illegal. Naturism in Brazil is often viewed as part of a broader movement toward freedom and a connection with nature, but it is still niche and not a central feature of Brazilian culture as a whole.

In cities like Rio de Janeiro, São Paulo, and others, nudist culture is less prominent, though you can find events, private spaces, and communities that cater to this lifestyle.

Legality and Safety

In Brazil, laws regarding nudity are complex as they blend cultural norms with legislative frameworks aimed at protecting public decency. While public nudity is not strictly illegal, it is governed by laws concerning "obscene acts" under the Brazilian Penal Code, which can lead to charges based on the context and location of the nudity. Enforcement can vary greatly across the country, often influenced by local community standards and perceptions of decency.

Nudism is accepted in certain designated areas, including about 35 locations where naturism is embraced, with eight officially recognized nude beaches: Praia do Pinho, Praia de Tambaba, Praia do Abricó, Praia de Massarandupió, Praia Brava (Cabo Frio), Olho de Boi, Praia de Barra Seca, and Praia de Pedras Altas. These areas demonstrate a growing acceptance for nudism. Additionally, the Brazilian Federal Constitution supports freedom of expression, which provides a basis for individuals advocating for their rights to engage in nudism. This situation creates a unique legal environment where personal discretion and societal acceptance are key, suggesting that while nudity may not be unlawful in specific contexts, it remains subject to regulation and community standards outside those areas.

Nudist beaches and resorts in Brazil are often well-regarded for their welcoming environments and emphasis on respect and privacy. Popular spots, particularly in areas known for naturism, tend to attract like-minded individuals, creating a relaxed and safe atmosphere. However, safety can vary by location, so it's important to consider a few key factors:

1. **Research the Destination:** Look for established nudist beaches or resorts with good reviews. Online forums and social media can provide insights from fellow travelers about safety and experiences.

2. **Local Regulations:** Familiarize yourself with the rules of the specific beach or resort. Some places may have designated areas for nudism, while others might be more lenient. Adhering to local customs helps ensure a positive experience.

3. **Travel in Groups:** If possible, visit with friends or fellow travelers. There's safety in numbers, and it can enhance the experience to share it with others.

4. **Stay Aware of Your Surroundings:** As with any beach or resort, it's wise to be aware of your environment. Keep personal belongings secure and be cautious of anyone acting suspiciously.

5. **Trust Your Instincts:** If a place feels uncomfortable or unwelcoming, it's okay to leave and seek another location.

6. **Respect Others' Privacy:** Nudist communities value consent and privacy. Always be respectful of others and avoid taking photos without permission.

Nudist Etiquette

Nudist culture in Brazil is centered around respect, personal boundaries, and a relaxed connection with nature. Understanding the etiquette and social norms at Brazil's nudist beaches are essential for a respectful and enjoyable experience. Here are some key points to consider:

- **Respect Personal Space:** Just because it's a nude beach doesn't mean it's acceptable to invade someone's personal space. Always maintain a respectful distance from others and avoid staring at or photographing fellow nudists without permission.

- **Towels for Hygiene:** Always bring a towel to sit on. It's customary to place your towel down on chairs, benches, or the sand when sitting, to ensure cleanliness and hygiene.

- **No Public Display of Affection:** Public displays of affection (PDA), such as passionate kissing or intimate touching, are generally discouraged on nude beaches. These actions may make others feel uncomfortable and are seen as inappropriate in these spaces.

- **Behavior and Discretion:** Nudist areas in Brazil are meant for relaxation and enjoying nature in a respectful, peaceful atmosphere. Keep your behavior calm and discreet, avoiding any inappropriate or overly attention-seeking actions.

- **Photography and Privacy:** Always ask for permission before taking photographs of others. Some beaches have strict rules against photography to protect privacy, and it's important to respect these guidelines.

- **Clothing for Entry and Exit:** While nudity is accepted in designated areas, it's expected that you wear clothing when entering or exiting the nudist area. This is especially true on beaches or resorts where nudist zones are clearly marked.

- **Respect Local Culture:** While nudism is allowed at certain beaches in Brazil, it is still a niche lifestyle, and the broader public may not be familiar with it. Always behave with the understanding that not everyone around you will share the same mindset.

 **General Questions**

1. *Is nudism legal in Brazil?* **Yes.** Nudism is not illegal in Brazil, but it is regulated. Public nudity outside of designated nudist areas or beaches is prohibited. However, Brazil recognizes several official nudist beaches where nudism is permitted, such as Praia do Pinho in Santa Catarina. These beaches are generally accepted by local authorities, and visitors can enjoy them without facing legal issues, as long as they adhere to the established norms.

2. *Can I get in trouble for practicing nudism at a non-designated beach in Brazil?* **Yes.** Practicing nudism at a non-designated beach or public area can lead to legal consequences in Brazil. Public nudity in non-nudist areas is generally prohibited under Brazil's public decency laws. Authorities may issue fines or even arrest individuals engaging in nudity outside of authorized spaces. It is important to always ensure you are at a recognized nudist beach to avoid legal trouble.

UNUSUAL LAWS

UNUSUAL LAWS

Overview[76]

Unusual laws can be fascinating glimpses into a culture's values and history. While most people are aware of common legal restrictions, it's often the strange and quirky laws that capture our attention. These regulations can range from the amusing to the absurd, reflecting the unique circumstances and traditions of a place. Whether they arise from historical events, societal norms, or simply peculiar local customs, unusual laws can provide insight into the quirks of human behavior and governance.

Brazil, like many countries, has a set of laws that can seem odd or humorous to outsiders. While some of these quirky regulations may not be actively enforced, they reflect the country's unique approach to public order, social norms, and culture. From bizarre rules about pets and public decency to odd restrictions on personal behavior, these laws offer a glimpse into the more light-hearted side of Brazilian governance. Whether you're a tourist or a resident, it's good to be aware of these quirky legal oddities to avoid surprise or embarrassment during your time in Brazil.

---

76 https://thebrazilbusiness.com/article/7-brazilian-unique-laws

Brazil's Unusual Laws and Associated Penalties

Brazil has a number of unique laws that reflect the country's vibrant culture, historical influences, and diverse legal system. While these laws are often not strictly enforced, penalties vary depending on the specific regulation, its enforcement, and the local authorities. Even though many of these laws may seem lighthearted or impractical, some can carry fines or other legal consequences.

For example, it's technically illegal to walk around with flip-flops in certain formal places, such as government offices or upscale businesses. Although enforcement is rare, you could be asked to leave or denied service, with no formal fine typically imposed. Another unusual regulation involves dancing or playing loud music after midnight in some cities. This can be considered a violation of local noise ordinances, and violators may face fines ranging from R$500 to R$2,000 (about US$100 to $400), with the possibility of police intervention if the disturbance continues.

Similarly, driving without a shirt may seem like an innocent choice, but it is considered a breach of public decency in Brazil. If caught, you could face a fine or be stopped by police. However, this law is rarely enforced unless combined with more disruptive behavior.

There is also a unique regulation by the Brazilian National Traffic Department that, in certain states, the driver's license number must be marked on the helmet of motorcyclists. This is a safety and identification measure designed to ensure that the rider is licensed and to provide easier identification in case of an accident or a traffic stop. If a motorcyclist does not have the required license number printed on their helmet, they can face fines and other penalties, such as having the motorcycle impounded or facing points on their driving record. And lastly, on a more social level, there's a light-hearted law requiring people to share their umbrella during the rain. While it's rarely enforced, refusing to share could lead to a scolding or reprimand, though there are no formal penalties for this one.

General Questions

1. *Is it true that in Brazil, you could be fined for driving with a dirty car?* **Yes.** In Brazil, there's a law in some states that fines people for driving a car that is excessively dirty, especially if it impedes the driver's ability to see through the windows or affects the vehicle's safety. While not universally enforced, it's meant to promote cleanliness and ensure safe driving conditions. If stopped by police and found to be in violation of this law, drivers could face fines or be asked to clean their vehicle before continuing their journey.

2. *What happens if you wear flip-flops in a government office in São Paulo?* In São Paulo, wearing flip-flops in government offices or other formal settings is actually illegal. The law is in place to maintain decorum and professionalism in public institutions. Flip-flops are seen as too casual and wearing them in these spaces could result in being fined or asked to leave the premises. While this may seem unusual, it reflects Brazil's appreciation for formal dress codes in work and public settings.

3. *Is it illegal to play soccer in some places in Brazil?* **Yes.** In some public spaces in Brazil, such as near airports or certain government buildings, playing soccer is technically illegal. This law was implemented to ensure safety and prevent accidents, especially in areas with heavy foot or vehicle traffic. Despite this, Brazil's national passion for soccer often leads to disregard of the law in informal settings, and fines are rarely issued unless it's deemed disruptive or dangerous.

TRAVELING SAFELY

IN THIS CHAPTER

- Ladies Traveling Solo
- Traveling as a Family
- Advice for All Travelers
- Do's and Don'ts While in Brazil

TRAVELING SAFELY

Ladies Traveling Solo[77]

Brazil is a country with a mixed reputation as a travel destination. It's celebrated for its vibrant culture, stunning landscapes, and diverse attractions, ranging from the beaches of Rio de Janeiro to the vast Amazon rainforest. However, concerns about safety, particularly in certain urban areas, have caused some hesitation among travelers. Crime, including theft and violence, is a well-documented issue that contributes to the perception of Brazil as potentially unsafe.

For solo female travelers, Brazil presents both enriching opportunities and considerable challenges, largely depending on the regions visited and the precautions taken. The country's warmth and inviting culture, alongside its natural beauty, can make it an appealing destination. However, Brazil faces persistent issues of gender-based violence and crime, which makes awareness and preparation crucial. Studies and travel reports suggest Brazil is among the higher-risk countries for women, with many ranking it second only to South Africa in terms of danger to solo female travelers. Many women report experiences of harassment, particularly in urban or less-populated areas, creating a sense of unease.

---

77 https://www.nomadher.com/blog-en/is-it-safe-to-travel-alone-as-a-woman-in-brazil#:~:text=There%20is%20a%20high%20rate,safe%2C%20just%20like%20I%20did

To ensure a safe and enjoyable journey, female travelers should plan meticulously and take essential safety precautions. Before setting off, it's important to research your destination thoroughly. Checking current travel advisories and local news can provide insight into potential risks, and talking to hotel or resort personnel—or trusted locals—about areas to avoid is also a wise step.

Once on the ground, sticking to well-populated areas, especially at night, is key. Isolated places, particularly after dark, can pose risks. When using taxis or ride-sharing services, always opt for licensed options, and confirm the route with the driver to ensure you're heading to the right location.

It's also important to share your itinerary and expected return times with a trusted friend or family member. Keeping someone informed is an added layer of security. Stay vigilant and trust your instincts. If something doesn't feel right, remove yourself from the situation. In some regions, dressing modestly can help avoid unwanted attention, as cultural norms can vary.

Lastly, learning a few basic Portuguese phrases can be useful, particularly in regions where Spanish is commonly spoken. By taking these precautions and planning ahead, female travelers can experience Brazil's beauty and culture while minimizing risks.

 You can read about more personal experiences of some solo female travelers touring Brazil at
https://www.wheregoesrose.com/solo-travel-brazil/ and
https://www.nomadher.com/blog-en/ is-it-safe-to-travel-alone-as-a-woman-in-brazil

Traveling as a Family

Traveling in Brazil as a family offers rich experiences with activities and destinations for all ages, from exploring the Amazon rainforest to visiting iconic sites like the Christ the Redeemer statue and Iguazu Falls. Brazilian culture values family, making it an accommodating destination with family-friendly attractions, restaurants, and hotels.

However, traveling with children requires careful planning. Families should choose family-friendly accommodations, plan for peak tourist seasons to avoid overcrowding, and stay informed about health recommendations like vaccinations. Essentials such as sunscreen, insect repellent, and a first aid kit are important for outdoor activities in diverse climates.

For safety, avoid areas with high crime rates and stay in well-populated, tourist-friendly locations like Copacabana or Florianopolis. Always have a contingency plan with emergency contacts, and avoid wearing flashy jewelry that could attract theft. In case of an emergency, **call the police at 190** or go to the nearest police station. Staying vigilant and teaching children to be aware of their surroundings will ensure a safe and enjoyable experience in Brazil.

Advice for All Travelers

There are certain places in Brazil that should be avoided, whether you are traveling by yourself or with family. If you still choose to travel to those high-risk places, be sure to take heightened precautions to avoid being a victim to crimes of opportunity.

The most violent areas of Brazil are in the north and northeast. In 2023, seven of the ten cities with the highest homicide rates were in the northeast. Feira da Santana was the most violent city in Brazil, with a murder rate of 58.69 per 100,000 people. Most cities in Brazil have areas known as favelas, or shantytowns. These densely populated informal neighborhoods are present in major cities and can be located near tourist areas. The safety in favelas is often unpredictable, and there have been incidents where tourists were shot after accidentally entering these areas, so you want to avoid these at any cost.

Safety Tips

Here are some essential tips for travelers visiting Brazil:

- **Stay Aware of Your Surroundings:** Brazil has areas with high crime rates, particularly in big cities. Always be aware of your surroundings, especially in crowded places, and avoid walking alone at night in unfamiliar or isolated areas.

- **Use Reliable Transportation:** Stick to registered taxis, ride-sharing apps like Uber, or public transport in well-lit, busy areas. Avoid accepting rides from unmarked vehicles.

- **Protect Your Belongings:** Petty theft, such as pickpocketing, is common in tourist areas. Keep valuables like passports, phones, and wallets secure, and avoid flashing expensive items.

- **Learn Basic Portuguese:** While many Brazilians in tourist spots may speak some English, it's helpful to learn a few basic phrases in Portuguese to communicate better, especially in less touristy areas. (For some common Portuguese phrases, refer to "Useful Brazilian Phrases" section at the end of the book).

- **Be Cautious with Water:** Tap water in Brazil is not always safe to drink in many areas. Stick to bottled water, especially in rural areas, and avoid consuming ice unless you're sure it's made from purified water.

- **Respect Local Customs:** Brazil has a diverse culture with different regional practices. Always show respect for local traditions and dress appropriately for different settings, especially in more conservative areas.

- **Stay Sun-Smart:** The sun in Brazil can be intense. Always wear sunscreen, a hat, and sunglasses, particularly if you're spending time on the beaches or in hot areas.

- **Understand the Climate:** Brazil's climate varies by region. Pack accordingly for both the heat and the occasional rain, especially in tropical areas like the Amazon or coastal cities.

- **Emergency Contacts:** Familiarize yourself with local emergency numbers—190 for police and 192 for medical emergencies—and know where the nearest hospital or embassy is.

- **Vaccinations:** Make sure you're up-to-date on routine vaccines before traveling, and check if you need any additional vaccinations, especially if traveling to the Amazon or rural areas. The yellow fever vaccination is often recommended.

 **Do's and Don'ts While in Brazil**

When visiting Brazil, understanding and respecting local customs can greatly enhance your experience. One essential "do" is to embrace the local language, Portuguese. While many Brazilians, especially in tourist areas, speak some English, making an effort to learn a few basic phrases in Portuguese can be appreciated and often reciprocated with kindness. Additionally, another important "do" is that visitors should partake in the vibrant culture of Brazil by exploring its culinary offerings, music, and dance. Attending a local festival, such as Carnaval, or trying traditional dishes like feijoada can provide a deeper connection to Brazilian culture. It is also advisable to dress appropriately for the occasion, as Brazilians tend to dress well, and adhering to local fashion can help in making a positive impression.

Conversely, there are some crucial "don'ts" that travelers should keep in mind to avoid cultural faux pas. For instance, visitors should never refer to Brazil's citizens as "Hispanic," as this term overlooks the unique cultural identity of Brazilians, who primarily speak Portuguese. Furthermore, it is important to "don't" discuss sensitive topics such as politics, poverty, or religion, as these subjects can spark heated debates and discomfort. Additionally, tourists should avoid displaying expensive belongings or large amounts of cash in public, as theft can be a concern in certain areas.

By following these do's and don'ts, visitors can enjoy a respectful, engaging, and memorable experience in Brazil, while also helping to bridge cultural differences.

CHAPTER 22
TOURIST TAXATION

TOURIST TAXATION

Tourist Taxes in Brazil[78]

In Brazil, several tourist taxes and fees may apply to travelers:

- The *ISS (Imposto Sobre Serviços)* is a municipal tax applied to hotel services and other services, typically ranging from 2 percent to 5 percent, depending on the city.

- A service fee may be added to restaurant and hotel bills, often around 10 percent, but it's optional and not mandatory.

- Some cities also charge a tourism fee, which funds local infrastructure and tourist promotions, usually between R$1.50 (US$0.26) and R$5.00 (US$0.87) per night. This fee is often included in hotel bills.

- A departure tax is included in the price of airline tickets and covers airport services.

- Some hotels may also charge a guest accommodation tax of 3 percent to 5 percent of the room rate, which supports local tourism development. It's advisable to check with accommodations about these additional charges.

- Additionally, some cities may charge an environmental fee, known as the *Taxa de Preservação Ambiental*, primarily in popular tourist destinations like Fernando de Noronha and Ilha Grande, designed to maintain the local ecosystem and promote sustainable tourism.

---

78 https://thebrazilbusiness.com/article/taxes-on-tourism-in-brazil

In terms of payment, tourists generally pay these taxes directly when receiving services. For instance, when booking accommodations or tours, the prices quoted by providers typically include the applicable taxes, ensuring transparency in the overall cost. In some situations, like dining in restaurants, the ISS may be included in the bill, though it is always advisable to inquire about the total cost beforehand.

As for international payments, Brazil has a diverse range of payment methods accepted, including credit cards, debit cards, and cash; however, it's wise to notify your bank about your travel plans to avoid any issues with international transactions. Familiarizing oneself with the local payment landscape and being prepared for service taxes can help ensure a smooth and enjoyable travel experience in Brazil.

 ## Law of the Land Hypothetical

HYPOTHETICAL: *Sarah, a tourist from the United States, is visiting Rio de Janeiro and staying at a beachfront hotel for a week. When she checks out, she notices a charge listed as "Tourism Fee" of R$3.00 (US$.052) per night. Surprised by this unexpected fee, she asks the hotel staff about it.*

Sarah is unsure about the tourism fee and wonders if it's something she's required to pay or if it's just an optional charge. Does she need to pay this fee?

ANSWER: **Yes.** *The Tourism Fee is a standard charge in several Brazilian cities, including Rio de Janeiro. It is used to fund local tourism projects, such as maintaining attractions and improving infrastructure. While this fee is not always mandatory (depending on where you are staying), it is a local tax that most hotels include in the final bill. The fee typically ranges from R$1.50 (US$0.26) to R$5.00 (US$0.87) per night, depending on the size and location of the hotel. In Sarah's case, the R$3.00 (US$0.52) per night fee is legitimate and is part of her* *hotel bill. Therefore, Sarah is required to pay this fee as part of her accommodation charges. It's always a good idea to confirm with the hotel about any additional charges like this when booking your stay to avoid surprises.*

CHAPTER 23

LONG-TERM STAYS

LONG-TERM STAYS

Overview

People choose to stay long-term in Brazil for a variety of compelling reasons that encompass economic, cultural, and quality-of-life factors. Economically, Brazil offers a dynamic market with robust private consumption and a labor market that has shown resilience, as evidenced by GDP growth rates of 2.9 percent in 2023, driven by strong consumer spending and social transfer policies. The country's diverse economy presents opportunities across multiple sectors, particularly in agriculture and services, appealing to both local and foreign investors.[79] Culturally, Brazil is renowned for its vibrant society characterized by rich traditions, music, festivals, and a strong sense of community that promotes deep familial and social bonds. Family remains central to Brazilian life, with strong expectations of loyalty and support among relatives. Furthermore, Brazil's varied climate offers something for everyone, from tropical beaches to temperate regions, allowing for outdoor activities year-round, which enhances the quality of life for residents. Lastly, the availability of universal healthcare through the *Unified Health System (SUS)* provides a safety net that attracts many who seek long-term stability and health security. These intertwined factors make Brazil an appealing option for individuals and families considering a long-term relocation.

---

79 https://www.worldbank.org/en/country/brazil/overview

Best Regions and Cities for Long-Term Living in Brazil

Brazil offers a range of cities and regions ideal for long-term living, each with its own unique appeal. São Paulo is the country's economic powerhouse, perfect for professionals seeking career opportunities, though it can be expensive. Rio de Janeiro combines vibrant culture, beautiful beaches, and a relaxed lifestyle, making it a top choice for expats, although it has a higher cost of living and security concerns in some areas. Florianópolis is renowned for its stunning natural beauty, laid-back atmosphere, and growing tech scene, offering a great work-life balance. Curitiba is known for its efficient public services, green spaces, and high quality of life, attracting families and those seeking a more organized, less chaotic urban experience. Belo Horizonte offers a lower cost of living and a rich cultural life, while Salvador offers a blend of historic charm, Afro-Brazilian culture, and affordable living. For a more tranquil, rural lifestyle, regions like Minas Gerais and parts of Santa Catarina are known for their peaceful environment and smaller cities with strong local communities. Each of these cities offers diverse opportunities and lifestyles, catering to a range of personal preferences and professional needs.

Living Cost in Brazil

Living costs in Brazil are generally much lower than in many Western countries, including the United States, although this varies by city and lifestyle. Larger cities like São Paulo and Rio de Janeiro can be expensive but are still more affordable than major Western cities. Smaller towns and rural areas offer even greater savings, making Brazil an appealing option for those looking to reduce living costs while maintaining a good quality of life. However, imported goods and specialized services can be more expensive, and the income disparity between Brazil and Western countries should also be considered.

For instance, rent for a one-bedroom apartment in central São Paulo or Rio de Janeiro ranges from US$500 to US$900 per month, while in smaller cities or rural areas, it can drop to US$160 to US$400. Basic groceries typically cost between US$120 and US$240 per month, and a mid-range three-course meal for two can range from US$30 to US$50.

Utilities (electricity, water, internet) for a standard one-bedroom apartment average US$60 to US$120 per month. Brazil's public healthcare system is free, but private health insurance is affordable, ranging from US$30 to US$160 per month depending on coverage.

Housing Options for Long-Term Stays

For visitors staying long-term in Brazil, there are a range of housing options depending on the city, budget, and lifestyle preferences. In major cities like São Paulo, Rio de Janeiro, and Brasília, visitors can find furnished apartments for rent, either in the form of short-term leases that can be extended or long-term rentals. These typically range from modern high-rise apartments in the city center to more affordable options in surrounding neighborhoods. Rent prices in these cities can be higher, especially in areas close to tourist attractions or business districts. In smaller cities and rural areas, housing options are generally more affordable, with visitors able to rent houses or apartments in quieter, more residential neighborhoods. Many landlords offer flexible leases, with some properties available for long-term stays on a yearly basis, and others offering rental agreements of six months or more.

For those seeking a more community-oriented experience, co-living spaces and shared apartments are increasingly popular, particularly in cities with large expat communities or a high number of digital nomads. Additionally, Airbnb and vacation rental platforms are common for those seeking furnished homes or apartments for longer stays, and many properties offer discounted rates for stays over a month. Depending on the location and type of property, visitors can expect to pay anywhere from US$300 to US$1,000 + per month for a one-bedroom apartment or house.

Transportation Options

Long-term visitors to Brazil have a variety of transportation options depending on their location. In major cities like São Paulo and Rio de Janeiro, public transportation is widely available, including buses, metro systems, and trains, with single fares ranging from US$0.80 to US$1.20. Taxis and ride-sharing services like Uber are also common, with relatively affordable fares starting around US$3 to US$5 for short trips. For those in smaller cities or rural areas, buses are the main form of public transport, though services can be less frequent. Renting a car is another popular option for exploring more remote regions or when public transport is limited, with rental prices starting around US$20 to US$40 per day. In many areas, walking and cycling are viable, especially in neighborhoods with good infrastructure or near the coast.

Healthcare Options for Long-Term Visitors[80]

There are several healthcare options, including both public and private systems. Brazil's public healthcare system (SUS) is free for residents and provides universal coverage, but it can be overcrowded and have long wait times, especially for non-emergency care. While long-term visitors are not eligible for SUS, they can access it in certain circumstances if they have a temporary visa. For those seeking faster and more personalized care, private healthcare is an option. Private hospitals and clinics in Brazil are generally of high quality, particularly in larger cities, and many doctors speak English. Visitors can choose from a range of private health insurance plans that cover medical expenses, hospital stays, and consultations, with premiums typically ranging from US$30 to US$160 per month, depending on the level of coverage. Many expats opt for private insurance to ensure access to quicker, higher-quality care. Some long-term visitors may also use international health insurance that covers Brazil, which can provide even more comprehensive coverage and global assistance. It's important for visitors to have health insurance, as out-of-pocket medical costs can be expensive, especially for major procedures or emergency care.

Language Considerations

For long-term visitors to Brazil, understanding the language landscape is essential, as Portuguese is the official and most widely spoken language across the country. Most Brazilians, particularly outside larger urban areas, have limited English proficiency, with estimates showing

---

80 https://www.april-international.com/en/destinations/america/
    health-insurance-in-brazil

that only about 5 percent of the population speaks English fluently.[81] As a result, not having a grasp of Portuguese can pose significant challenges in daily interactions, such as reading signs, understanding menus, and navigating public transportation systems. Consequently, learning some basic Portuguese phrases and vocabulary can greatly enhance a visitor's experience, facilitating smoother interactions and fostering connections with locals. Such efforts are not just practical but also demonstrate respect for Brazilian culture and its people, often leading to friendlier and more meaningful exchanges.

Long-term visitors to Brazil should be aware of regional variations in language, including distinct dialects and informal expressions that vary between states. Additionally, many residents may speak other languages such as Spanish, Italian, or indigenous languages, further diversifying the linguistic landscape. To navigate these differences, visitors are encouraged to use language learning apps, take local language courses, and immerse themselves in environments that promote conversational practice.

Brazilian Visa Categories and Residency Requirements

Brazil offers a variety of long-term visa categories for individuals wishing to stay in the country for extended periods. Below is a detailed breakdown of the main long-term visa categories, along with their requirements:

1. Temporary Visas (Visto Temporário)

These visas are typically valid for 1 to 2 years and can be extended under certain conditions. They are granted for a variety of purposes, including work, study, family reunion, and investment.

---

81   https://www.marquitastravels.com/english-in-brazil/

a. Work Visa (Visto de Trabalho)

Requirements:

- Job offer from a Brazilian employer (must be approved by the Ministry of Labor).
- Proof of your professional qualifications or experience.
- Relevant employment contract.
- Proof of income or financial stability.
- Application submitted through the Brazilian consulate in your home country or via the Ministry of Justice in Brazil.

b. Student Visa (Visto de Estudante)

Requirements:

- Enrollment in an accredited educational institution in Brazil (e.g., university or language school).
- Proof of sufficient financial resources to support yourself while studying.
- Proof of health insurance.
- Payment of the visa application fee.
- Visa can be granted for the duration of the course.

c. Family Reunion Visa (Visto de Reagrupamento Familiar)

Requirements:

- Proof of a family relationship with a Brazilian citizen or legal resident (e.g., marriage certificate or birth certificate).
- The Brazilian citizen or resident must demonstrate financial capability to support the foreign family member.
- Completed application form and payment of fees.

- Proof of clean criminal record from both your home country and Brazil.
- Family members eligible for this visa include spouses, children under 18, and sometimes parents.

d. Investor Visa (Visto de Investidor)

Requirements:

- A minimum investment (usually BRL 150,000 ($25,980 USD) or more) in a Brazilian business or project.
- The business must create jobs or positively impact the Brazilian economy.
- Proof of the investment and business plan.
- Evidence of financial capacity to support yourself and your dependents in Brazil.
- This visa is granted for 2 years, with the possibility of extension.

e. Volunteer Visa (Visto de Voluntário)

Requirements:

- Proof of participation in a recognized non-profit organization or volunteer program.
- Confirmation that the volunteer work will be unpaid.
- Proof of health insurance and sufficient financial resources.
- The visa can be issued for up to 1 year, with a possibility of extension.

f. Digital Nomad Visa (Visto de Nômade Digital)

Requirements:

- Proof of remote employment or freelance work for foreign companies.

- Minimum monthly income (typically around USD $1,500 or more).
- Proof of health insurance coverage.
- No involvement in local employment or direct income generation in Brazil.
- The visa is valid for 1 year, with the possibility of renewal.

2. Permanent Visas (Visto Permanente)

Permanent visas allow individuals to live in Brazil indefinitely. These visas are available under certain conditions, such as family reunion, investment, and skilled work.

a. Marriage or Family Reunion Visa

Requirements:

- A Brazilian spouse, child, or parent must sponsor the applicant.
- Proof of the relationship, such as marriage certificates or birth certificates.
- Evidence of financial support (sponsor must demonstrate the ability to financially support the foreign national).
- Criminal background checks from the home country and Brazil.
- If married to a Brazilian citizen, the waiting period for applying for permanent residency is usually 2 years. For other family members, it may take longer (generally 2-5 years).

b. Retirement Visa (Visto de Aposentado)

Requirements:

- Proof of stable income (usually a pension or annuity) of at least R$6,000 (US$1,039.20) per month (can vary by region and consulate).
- Health insurance covering the applicant in Brazil.

- Proof of identity and criminal background check.
- Application through the Brazilian consulate or Ministry of Justice.
- Retirees can apply for this visa even if they are not employed in Brazil.

c. Investor Visa (Visto de Investidor)

Requirements:

- A higher financial investment than the temporary version, generally around R$500,000 (US$86,600) or more.
- The investment must be in a productive business (e.g., job creation, new business ventures).
- The business must be operational and have a positive impact on the Brazilian economy.
- The visa can lead to permanent residency after a period of compliance with investment conditions (usually 2 years or more).

d. Highly Skilled Worker Visa (Visto de Trabalhador Qualificado)

Requirements:A job offer from a Brazilian company in a sector that requires highly specialized skills (e.g., engineering, healthcare, IT).

- Relevant qualifications, education, or experience in the field.
- The employer must demonstrate that no Brazilian worker is qualified for the position.
- The visa is typically granted for skilled professionals in high-demand fields.

e. Naturalization

Requirements:

- After living in Brazil for a certain period, foreign nationals can apply for naturalization (Brazilian citizenship).

- For those married to Brazilian citizens, naturalization is available after 2 years of residence in Brazil.

- For other foreigners, naturalization is available after 4 years of legal residency (can be reduced to 1 year if you have Brazilian children).

- The applicant must show that they have legal status, stable income, and no serious criminal record in Brazil.

Visa Costs

The cost of visas in Brazil varies based on the type of visa, the applicant's nationality, and whether the application is processed in Brazil or through a consulate abroad.

For a tourist visa, fees generally range from US$40 to US$160, depending on the nationality of the applicant. Temporary visas, such as work, study, or family reunion visas, typically cost between US$50 and US$200. Permanent visas, including investment and family reunion visas, usually range from US$100 to US$500. Additionally, residence and naturalization applications may cost between US$100 and US$300. Extra consular fees may apply for processing or document legalization. The total cost of a visa depends on the type, processing location, and specific requirements.

 For more information on specific visa-related fees, please visit **https://www.gov.br/mre/pt-br/consulado-washington/consulate-general-of-brazil-in-washington-dc/visa-fees**

 **General Questions**

1. *What happens if I overstay my visa?* Overstaying a visa in Brazil can lead to several serious consequences. First, individuals who exceed their authorized stay may face fines, which can vary depending on the length of the overstay, with amounts reaching approximately R$8,200 [US$1,500] for stays longer than 90 days.[82] Furthermore, overstaying can complicate future travel plans, as it may result in deportation and a potential ban on re-entering Brazil for a specified period. In extreme cases, individuals may be detained by immigration authorities until the matter is resolved or until an exit from the country is arranged. Hence, it is crucial for visitors to adhere to their visa conditions to avoid these punitive measures.

2. *What income requirements are there for a long-stay visa in Brazil?* Income requirements for long-stay visas in Brazil vary based on the type of visa. For example, a retirement visa typically requires proof of a stable income, usually between US$1,500 to US$2,000 per month (or its equivalent in Brazilian reais). For a work visa, you must have a job offer from a Brazilian employer who can demonstrate the ability to pay your salary according to Brazilian labor laws, with salaries generally needing to meet the minimum wage or higher for the type of work. For an investment visa, applicants generally need to invest a minimum amount, often R$500,000 (about US$100,000), and create jobs for Brazilian citizens. The specific income or financial requirements depend on the visa category and individual circumstances.

---

82 https://www.gov.br/pf/pt-br/assuntos/imigracao/controle-migratorio/step_by_step_guide.pdf

3. *If I want to stay in Brazil long-term and work, should I apply for a work permit before arriving in Brazil?* **Yes**. If you want to work in Brazil long-term, you must apply for a work visa before arriving in the country. Brazil requires foreigners to have a valid work permit or employment visa to legally work. This visa is typically sponsored by a Brazilian employer who must prove that there are no qualified Brazilian candidates for the position. Once granted, a work visa allows you to live and work in Brazil for the duration of your employment contract. Arriving in Brazil without the appropriate work visa and seeking employment while on a tourist visa can lead to legal issues, including deportation.

 **Takeaways**

- **Visa Regulations:** Ensure you're aware of Brazil's visa requirements, as overstaying can lead to fines or deportation. U.S. citizens will need a visa from 2025.

- **Healthcare:** Brazil offers free public healthcare (SUS), but private insurance is recommended for quicker access to medical services.

- **Language:** Portuguese is the primary language; learning basic phrases is essential for smooth communication and cultural immersion.

- **Cultural Norms:** Embrace Brazilian customs like warm greetings, lively conversations, and the importance of food and soccer. Be aware of regional differences.

- **Safety:** Crime can be a concern in cities. Stay in safe areas, avoid showing valuables, and use trusted transport options.

CIVIL LITIGATION

CIVIL LITIGATION[83]

Overview

Civil litigation provides a mechanism for resolving disputes, ensuring that travelers have a way to seek justice if legal issues arise while visiting another country. It helps them understand their rights and obligations under local laws, which may differ from those in their home country. The civil litigation system offers a formal process for addressing conflicts, such as contract disputes or personal injury claims, and can deter unfair practices by encouraging businesses to comply with legal standards. It also allows individuals to seek financial recourse for damages or losses and helps protect them from potential exploitation by local entities. Overall, understanding civil litigation enhances a visitor's experience and safety while traveling.

Personal Injury Claims and Compensation Law

Personal Injury Law in Brazil operates under a comprehensive civil framework designed to ensure adequate treatment and compensation for individuals harmed due to negligence or wrongful actions. This legal structure assists victims of accidents, medical malpractice, and

---

83 https://iclg.com/practice-areas/
    litigation-and-dispute-resolution-laws-and-regulations/brazil

workplace injuries, highlighting the importance of understanding the claims process to secure damages.

The foundation for personal injury claims is rooted in the principles of civil liability outlined in the Brazilian Civil Code. To establish a successful claim, the injured party must prove that the defendant acted negligently or intentionally caused harm, that damage occurred, and that a causal link exists between the two. Brazil's fault-based system allows for full compensation for damages without limitations common in other jurisdictions, enabling victims to seek restitution for various injuries, including those from road traffic accidents and medical malpractice.

Road traffic accidents are prevalent sources of personal injury claims, allowing victims to receive prompt compensation if the responsible driver is found liable. Brazilian law recognizes moral damages related to psychological impacts and encompasses compensation for pain and suffering, medical expenses, and lost income. The potential for re-evaluation of compensation arises if a victim's condition worsens over time, reflecting the complexities of long-term recovery. Insurance plays a vital role in streamlining the compensation process, facilitating direct claims against insurers. However, disputes regarding coverage can arise, necessitating legal expertise to address any claims-related challenges.

The process typically starts with negotiations, and if unsuccessful, it proceeds to court.

How to File a Civil Claim

Filing a civil claim in Brazil involves several crucial steps that are governed by the Brazilian Code of Civil Procedure. Initially, the plaintiff must prepare an initial complaint, which should include detailed information about the parties involved, the basis of the claim, the facts leading to the dispute, and the specific remedies being sought from the court. This initial petition must also be supported by all relevant documentation as evidence, such as contracts, witness statements, and expert reports, to substantiate the claims. After the complaint is drafted, it needs to be submitted to the competent court, where the jurisdiction is determined based on the nature of the claim and the geographic location associated with the case. Following the submission, the court will review the complaint to ensure it meets legal requirements and, if accepted, issue a summons for the defendant to respond.

Once the court has issued the summons, the defendant typically has a period of 15 business days to file their defense or counterclaim. The process may involve various stages, including preliminary hearings for conciliation, evidentiary phases, and ultimately a judgment phase where the court issues its decision based on the evidence presented by both parties. It is essential for plaintiffs to be aware of the time limits for filing claims, as Brazilian law generally imposes strict statutes of limitations that may vary depending on the type of civil action. Overall, navigating the civil claims process in Brazil requires not only an understanding of legal principles but also careful attention to procedural details to ensure that claims are appropriately filed and adequately supported.

How to File a Criminal Claim

Filing a criminal claim in Brazil involves several key procedures that must be adhered to in order to ensure the claim is valid and actionable. Firstly, the victim or their representative must file the complaint with the relevant authorities, typically the Public Ministry (*Ministério Público*), which has the responsibility to accept or reject the charge within a specified timeframe, as outlined in Brazilian legal procedures. The initial filing requires that all necessary documentation and evidence related to the claimed offense be gathered and submitted for consideration. Specifically, the claim must include a detailed description of the incident, information about the accused, any corroborating evidence, and, if applicable, witness statements to substantiate the allegations. This procedural framework aims to uphold the fair administration of justice while granting individuals the right to seek redress.

Moreover, it is essential to understand the repercussions of filing a criminal claim in Brazil, particularly regarding false or malicious accusations. The Brazilian Penal Code criminalizes the act of bringing a malicious claim, which may lead to significant penalties for individuals found guilty of such offenses.[84] The justice system places the burden of proof primarily on the claimant, indicating that they must substantiate their allegations with credible evidence while also adhering to the standards of proof within the judicial process. Consequently, individuals must approach the filing of a criminal claim with diligence, ensuring that all legal protocols are followed and recognizing the potential legal consequences of unfounded allegations. This comprehensive approach safeguards the integrity of the justice system and deters the misuse of legal channels for false claims.

Service of Documents[85]

The service of documents in Brazil typically involves a formal procedure governed by both international and national regulations, including the Hague Service Convention of which Brazil is a signatory. For initiating legal proceedings, it is essential to serve documents such as summons or complaints to the involved parties, following a specific sequence mandated by Brazilian law.

The first step is to submit a request to Brazil's Central Authority, which cannot be done by postal mail from abroad; a representative in Brazil must file the request. After submission, the Central Authority processes the documents and forwards them to the appropriate judicial authority for further action. It's crucial that all documents be translated into Portuguese and certified for compliance with local regulations; failure to do so may result in the rejection of the service request. Informal service methods are not recognized under Brazilian law, emphasizing the need for adherence to formal procedures to ensure all parties receive adequate legal notice.

Statute of Limitations

Brazilian law categorizes statutes of limitations based on the nature of the underlying claim. For instance, the general limitation period for civil

---

84   https://www.countryreports.org/country/Brazil/criminal-penalties.htm

85   https://www.haguelawblog.com/2017/06/serve-process-brazil/

actions is three years from the date the right to bring an action arose, while specific claims, such as those related to contracts, might have different periods, extending up to ten years.

The Brazilian Penal Code also establishes time limits for criminal prosecution, which vary significantly based on the severity of the crime, typically ranging from three to twenty years. The limits are particularly stringent for serious offenses like homicide, where the statute of limitations may last up to twenty years.

Moreover, certain exceptions exist that can interrupt or suspend the statute of limitations. For example, if a defendant leaves the country, the limitation period can be paused until their return. In tax law, the statute of limitations for tax disputes is generally up to five years from the occurrence of the infringement; however, this period may be extended under specific circumstances.

 ## Getting Married in Brazil[86]

Visitors can get married in Brazil, but there are specific legal requirements and documentation that must be fulfilled. To initiate the marriage process, foreign nationals will need to present a valid passport, which serves as the primary form of identification throughout the marriage procedure, regardless of their home country. Additionally, a certificate of civil status, indicating that the person is not currently married, must be obtained from their home country and legalized by the Brazilian Consulate or Embassy. For those who are divorced, documentation proving the final divorce decree is necessary, along with a legalized death certificate for widows or widowers if applicable.

The marriage itself must occur at a local notary public office, known as a *"Cartório,"* where both parties are required to fill out forms and complete the registration process. This entails choosing a marital

---

86 https://www.netherlandsworldwide.nl/marry/brazil

regime, which determines how assets will be managed and distributed before and during marriage. Furthermore, a waiting period known as *"Proclamas"* is mandatory, during which the couple's intent to marry must be publicly announced, followed by a registration of the marriage, which is valid for 90 days from the date of the announcement. In conclusion, while getting married in Brazil is feasible for visitors, it necessitates careful preparation and compliance with the outlined legal procedures to ensure a valid marriage recognition.

Additionally, Brazil recognizes civil union (*uniões estáveis*) and grants them legal recognition and rights similar to marriage. To formalize a civil union, couples do not need to go through the same legal formalities as marriage, but they may need to register their union in a notary office to ensure it is officially recognized.

The minimum age for marriage is set at 18 years old, according to the Civil Code of 2002. However, individuals who are 16 or 17 years old can marry with the consent of their parents or legal representatives. Furthermore, children under 16 are prohibited from marrying under any circumstances following a recent law change that tightened restrictions on child marriage.[87]

 **Law of the Land Hypothetical**

HYPOTHETICAL: *Maria, a U.S. citizen, was in a car accident in Brazil on July 1, 2022, where another driver was at fault. She suffered injuries, incurred medical expenses of R$30,000 (US$5,196), and lost wages of R$15,000 (US$2,598). Maria returned to the U.S. and delayed filing a claim. In August 2025, she consults a lawyer about filing a personal injury lawsuit. What is the statute of limitations for Maria*

---

87 https://plan-international.org/news/2019/03/22/
brazil-bans-child-marriage-for-under-16s

to file a personal injury claim in Brazil? Can she still file the lawsuit after more than three years have passed?

ANSWER: *In Brazil, the statute of limitations for personal injury claims is three years from the date of the accident or when the injured party becomes aware of the damage and the responsible party. Since Maria knew the responsible driver and her injuries right after the accident, the three-year period likely started on July 1, 2022. This means she has until July 1, 2025, to file a lawsuit. After that, the claim is generally barred, unless there are exceptional circumstances that could extend the period. Therefore, Maria may have missed the deadline to file her lawsuit.*

CHAPTER 25
OTHER THINGS TO KNOW

OTHER THINGS TO KNOW

Tourists and Street Hustling

Street hustling is a common phenomenon in Brazil, especially in major cities and tourist hotspots, where street vendors or hustlers often target locals and tourists alike. These hustlers may offer various goods or services, and while many are legitimate, some may be scams designed to exploit unsuspecting individuals. Especially popular tourist destinations and large urban centers like Rio de Janeiro, São Paulo, Salvador, and Foz do Iguaçu see high levels of street hustling, where tourists are often approached by hustlers selling overpriced items or offering dubious services.

 **Common Scams to Be Aware of**

- **Overpriced Goods and Services:** Tourists are often charged significantly higher prices for goods like souvenirs, drinks, or services like street performances. Always check prices before accepting any offer.

- **Fake or Low-Quality Products:** Hustlers may sell counterfeit items or products of inferior quality, such as electronics that don't work or counterfeit watches.

- **"Free" Gifts or Services:** Some hustlers will offer "free" services, such as jewelry or friendship bracelets, and then demand an inflated tip afterward, often using intimidation or emotional pressure.

- **Fake "Tour Guides":** Unofficial guides might offer tours at inflated rates or take tourists to less interesting or safe places, often leading to situations where tourists feel pressured to pay more.

- **Pickpocketing and Distraction Scams:** Common in crowded places, scammers might use distraction techniques, such as pretending to ask for directions or engaging in a street performance, to pickpocket tourists.

- **Fake Tickets or Services:** Some hustlers sell fake tickets to events, attractions, or public transport, often targeting tourists in busy areas.

While street hustling is not regulated, enforcement varies, and tourists should remain cautious, check prices before accepting offers, and avoid engaging with unsolicited services.

Safety Concerns and Practical Tips

While street hustling is common in Brazil, especially in tourist areas, there are several safety concerns for visitors. Tourists can become victims of scams, theft, or aggressive sales tactics. Street hustlers may pressure tourists into paying more for goods or services, or use distraction techniques to steal valuables. In some cases, scams may escalate into confrontational situations where tourists feel intimidated into handing over money.

To deal with street hustling effectively, tourists should remain vigilant in crowded tourist hotspots. It's essential to avoid engaging with unsolicited offers, especially when goods or services appear too good to be true. Always negotiate prices upfront with street vendors and avoid accepting "free" gifts or services, as these are often followed by demands for tips. When dealing with street performers or guides, ensure they are legitimate and agreed upon in advance. It's also important to keep valuables secured and avoid displaying large amounts of cash or expensive items in public. Tourists should stay aware of their surroundings, particularly in busy markets or areas with large crowds, as pickpockets may use distraction techniques. Lastly, if a scam or unsafe situation arises, it's advisable to remain calm, walk away, and seek help from local authorities or other tourists if necessary.

 ## In the Event of Death

Experiencing the death of a loved one or a friend while traveling in Brazil can be an incredibly distressing situation, and it requires immediate and careful steps to manage the circumstances effectively. The first action to take is to notify local authorities, typically the police, who will need to investigate the circumstances surrounding the death, particularly if it occurred under unusual conditions. It is essential to document the scene and gather any vital details that can assist in the investigation. Following the notification of local authorities, contacting the deceased's home country's consulate or embassy in Brazil is crucial for support and guidance through this intricate process.

Once local authorities have been notified and the necessary documentation processes have begun, the family or friends of the deceased must make arrangements concerning the body. This may involve choosing whether to have the body buried in Brazil or repatriated to the deceased's home country. If repatriation is the desired option, consulting with funeral homes experienced in international cases is vital, as they can facilitate the complicated procedures associated with transporting human remains. This includes ensuring proper embalming of the body, securing the necessary permits, and coordinating transport logistics.

Throughout this challenging experience, support from the consulate or embassy can be invaluable, providing not only logistical assistance but also emotional resources such as grief counseling for those coping with their loss while away from home. Recognizing the problem and acting quickly can significantly ease the process during such a poignant time.

 For more information on repatriating remains, contact the CDC's *Division of Global Migration and Quarantine* at 770-488-7100, or email dgmqpolicyoffice@cdc.gov.

Experiencing Financial Hardship

If you are a U.S. citizen facing financial hardship while traveling in Brazil, your first step should be to contact the nearest U.S. embassy or consulate. You can also reach out to the U.S. Department of State's Office of Overseas Citizens Services at +1 202-501-4444 for assistance. They can help you by arranging emergency funds from family, your bank, or employer, or in some cases, wiring funds directly to you. The embassy may also assist in securing a repatriation loan to cover travel, food, lodging, and medical expenses. Commercial money transfer services like Western Union and MoneyGram are widely available and can help you receive funds quickly. In emergency situations, selling personal valuables may provide immediate cash.

To stretch your remaining funds, consider staying in affordable hostels, shopping at local markets, and using Brazil's extensive public transportation system. If permitted by your visa, you may explore short-term work opportunities, such as teaching English or freelance jobs. Contact your bank or credit card provider to inquire about emergency funds or increasing ATM withdrawal limits. Always remain cautious of scams and be vigilant with your financial transactions. Once stabilized, set a daily budget and keep detailed records of all expenses and communications.

In Brazil, there are several resources that may help tourists facing financial hardship:

- **Tourism Information Centers** in major cities can provide details on affordable accommodation, local meals, and available charity services.

- **Emergency Assistance:** Organizations like the Brazilian Red Cross, local Social Services, or community centers may offer help with food, shelter, and transportation.

- **NGOs** (Non-Governmental Offices) and **Charities** such as Associação de Assistência à Criança Deficiente (AACD) and others offer food and emergency aid.

- **Crowdfunding** platforms like GoFundMe can be used to seek financial assistance from family, friends, or even strangers.

- **Emergency Loans:** Some Brazilian banks may offer short-term loans with basic documentation like proof of ID and travel plans.

- **Discounted Transportation:** In certain cases, local transport providers may offer discounted or free rides for individuals in need.

- **Local Community Networks:** Expat groups, online forums, and social media communities may provide valuable advice or direct financial assistance.

Remember to always stay in contact with the embassy and keep a close eye on your finances during difficult times abroad.

General Questions

1. *What vaccinations do I need for Brazil?* There is a risk of malaria in some areas of Brazil, so it's essential to consult with your doctor before traveling to determine whether you need antimalarial medication based on your destination. Additionally, cases of the Zika virus have been reported in the country, so it's crucial to take precautions against mosquito bites. To protect yourself, use a strong insect repellent containing at least 50% DEET and consider sleeping under a mosquito net at night, especially in areas where mosquitoes are more prevalent. Taking these steps will help reduce the risk of both malaria and Zika virus. [88]

---

88 https://www.onthegotours.com/us/Brazil/Travel-tips-and-useful-info

2. *How to eat safely in Brazil?* Brazilians are experts at cooking meat, so you can generally expect well-prepared dishes. However, it's important to be cautious with salads and unpeeled fruit, as they may have been washed in contaminated water and could cause illness. Street food is usually safe, but it's wise to avoid anything that appears to have been left out in the sun for too long.[89]

3. *Is it standard to tip in Brazil?* Given that wages are generally very low in Brazil, many workers in the service industry rely on tips to make up their salary. Ten percent is often added to the bill in restaurants, but if the service has been particularly good, there is no harm in leaving a little extra on the table. You should also consider tipping hotel staff, taxi drivers, and tour guides. For taxi drivers, it is acceptable to simply round up the fare. For hotel staff, you only need to tip the equivalent of a dollar or two per day. If the tour guide has been exceptionally good, then US$10 per day is an appropriate tip.

---

89 https://www.onthegotours.com/us/Brazil/Travel-tips-and-useful-info

QUICK REFERENCE GUIDE

- Quick Chapter References to Important Topics

QUICK REFERENCE GUIDE

Crime in Brazil

Are there particular areas that I should avoid as a tourist?

Yes. There are several cities where it is inadvisable to travel to. These cities include, but are not limited to, Brasilia, Rio de Janeiro, and San Paulo. *For more details, see Chapter 3.*

Drug Offenses

Is the possession of marijuana legal?

Yes. Personal use small amounts of marijuana have been de-criminalized.

Is the possession of cocaine legal?

No. *For more details, see Chapter 4.*

Alcohol-Related Offenses

What is the legal drinking age?

18 is the legal drinking age.

What is the legal blood alcohol limit?

> Brazil has a "dry law" indicating a nearly zero alcohol tolerance law regarding driving. The tolerated blood alcohol limit is **0.2g/l**, to allow for alcoholic mouthwashes or certain medicines. *For more details, see Chapter 5.*

Firearm & Ammunition Offenses

Can I possess a handgun in Brazil?

> **No,** not without prior authorization from the relevant authorities. *For more details, see Chapter 6.*

Prostitution

Is prostitution legal?

> **Yes.** Prostitution itself is legal in Brazil, but activities such as pimping, running brothels, and trafficking are illegal. *For more details, see Chapter 7.*

LGBTQ

Is homosexuality legal?

> **Yes**, homosexuality is legal in Brazil.

Are same sex public displays of affection legal?

> **Yes**, same-sex public displays of affection are legal in Brazil. Same-sex couples have the same rights as heterosexual couples, and public displays of affection are generally accepted, though, as with any country, respect for local customs and sensitivities is advised. *For more details, see Chapter 8.*

Arrested in Brazil

Would I be entitled to bail if I'm arrested?

Yes. Bail is available for most crimes but is granted infrequently.

Will a lawyer be provided to me if I cannot afford one?

Yes, if the accused cannot afford an attorney, the judge will appoint a public defender. *For more details, see Chapter 10.*

Helping a Friend or Relative Imprisoned in Brazil

Can I send money to a friend or relative imprisoned in Brazil?

Yes, the United State Consulate can assist in establishing an OCS Trust to transfer money to a prisoner in Brazil. *For more details, see Chapter 12.*

Crime Victim Assistance

Can a victim of a crime be legally compensated?

In Brazil, only domestic violence victims are legally guaranteed compensation from the aggressor to pay for medical bills.

Does the Brazilian government offer assistance for family members of homicide victims?

Yes, the Brazilian government provides assistance to family members of homicide victims, though the support can vary depending on the state or municipality. This assistance may include emotional and psychological support through public health services, legal aid for navigating the criminal justice system, and sometimes financial support for funeral expenses. *For more details, see Chapter 14.*

Police

Is there a number to dial for a police emergency in Brazil?

Yes, dial 190 in the event of a police emergency. *For more details, see Chapter 15.*

How to Get Legal Help in Brazil

Is there a resource in Brazil to find legal representation?

Yes, visit **https://br.usembassy.gov/u-s-citizen-services/attorneys/** for a list of attorneys in Brazil that speak English.

Is pro bono legal representation assistance offered in Brazil?

Yes, Brazilian law guarantees that anyone who is not financially able to hire the services of a lawyer and pay for legal proceedings is entitled to free legal aid. *For more details, see Chapter 16.*

Foreign Embassies in Brazil

Are there foreign embassies in Brazil?

Yes, the Brazilian capital Brasilia hosts 131 embassies, and in addition, there are 536 consulates and three other representations in Brazil.

Is there a website to locate embassies in Brazil?

Yes, **https://www.embassypages.com/brazil**. *For more details, see Chapter 16.*

Medical Facilities & Hospitals

Is there a number I can call in Brazil for ambulance and fire emergencies?

Yes, dial **192** for ambulance, and **193** fire emergencies.

If I am injured while on vacation in Brazil, are there hospitals that are recommended for tourists?

> **Yes**, there are hospitals in Brazil that cater to tourists, especially in major cities and tourist areas. Some recommended ones include **Hospital Israelita Albert Einstein** and **Hospital das Clínicas in São Paulo**, and **Copa D'Or Hospital** in Rio de Janeiro. These hospitals often have international patient services and English-speaking staff. It's advisable to have travel insurance that covers medical expenses. *For more details, see Chapter 17.*

Driving in Brazil

Which side of the road do I drive on in Brazil?

> Cars are driven on the **right side** of the road.

Can I use my driver's license from my home country to drive in Brazil?

> **Yes**, foreigners are allowed to drive in Brazil for up to 180 days after entering the country if they have a valid driver's license from their home country. *For more details, see Chapter 18.*

Nude Beaches & Clothing-Optional Resorts

Is public nudity legal on the beaches?

> Only on specified beaches. *For more details, see Chapter 19.*

Tourist Taxation

Is there a tourist tax in Brazil?

> **Yes**, tourists in Brazil are subject to ISS collection.

What affects the amount of tourist tax I have to pay?

> The amount of tourist tax can vary based upon the length of your hotel stay in Brazil. *For more details, see Chapter 22.*

Long-Term Stays

Do I need to return to my home country to apply for a work permit in Brazil?

Yes.

As an American, how long can I stay in Brazil without a visa?

As an American, you can stay in Brazil for up to **90 days** without a visa for tourism, business, or transit purposes. This period can be extended for an additional 90 days, but the total stay cannot exceed 180 days in a 12-month period. After that, you would need to leave the country and reapply for entry. *For more details, see Chapter 23.*

In the Event of Death

What documents would an embassy need regarding the death of a tourist?

In the event of a tourist's death in Brazil, the embassy typically requires the death certificate, identification, autopsy report (if applicable), next of kin details, proof of residence, and insurance documents to assist with repatriation and legal matters. *For more details, see Chapter 25.*

U.S. Consulate Assistance

Are there any limitations to the consulate assistance I can receive while in Brazil?

Yes, consulate assistance in Brazil has limitations. The consulate cannot intervene in legal matters, provide financial support, or cover personal debts. They can assist with documentation, repatriation, emergency contact services, and legal referrals, but they cannot offer legal representation or solve criminal or civil disputes. *For more details, see Chapter 14.*

EMERGENCY/IMPORTANT CONTACT NUMBERS IN BRAZIL

 Please consider adding these numbers to your phone contacts prior to traveling to Brazil in case of an emergency.

AMBULANCE: 192

ANONYMOUS CRIME REPORTING: 181

CIVIL DEFENSE: 199

CIVIL POLICE: 197

FEDERAL HIGHWAY POLICE: 191

FEDERAL POLICE: 194

FIREFIGHTERS: 193

HOSPITAL: 136 (YOU WILL BE DIRECTED TO THE LOCAL HOSPITAL)

LOCAL HOSPITAL (E.G., HOSPITAL COPA D'OR, RIO DE JANEIRO):
+55 21 2539-5333

POLICE: 190

TOURIST POLICE: 147

U.S. CONSULATE IN RIO DE JANEIRO: +55 21 3823-2000

U.S. CONSULATE IN SÃO PAULO: +55 11 3250-5000

U.S. EMBASSY IN BRASILIA: +55 61 3312-7000

USEFUL PORTUGUESE PHRASES

GREETINGS

HI/HELLO – Olá

GOOD MORNING – Bom dia

GOOD AFTERNOON – Boa tarde

GOOD NIGHT – Boa noite

GOODBYE – Adeus

MAGIC WORDS

PLEASE – Por favor

THANK YOU – Obrigado/a (use "obigrado" if you're male, "obrigada" if you're female

YOU'RE WELCOME – De nada

CHEERS! – Saúde!

EXCUSE ME – Desculpa

YES/NO – Sim/não

GETTING AROUND

WHERE IS THE BATHROOM? – Onde fica o banheiro?

WHAT TIME IS IT? – Que horas são?

HOW DO I GET TO...? – Como eu chego a...?

WHERE DOES THIS TRAIN/BUS GO? – Onde vai esse trem/ônibus?

RESTAURANT – Restaurante

HOW MUCH DOES THIS COST? – Quanto custa isso?

TRAIN/METRO STATION – Estação de trem/metro

COMMUNICATION

DO YOU SPEAK ENGLISH? – Você fala inglês?

I DO NOT UNDERSTAND – Não entendo

I DON'T SPEAK PORTUGUESE – Não falo português

I DON'T KNOW – Não sei

EMERGENCY

HELP! – Socorro!

CALL AN AMBULANCE! – Chame uma ambulância!

I NEED A DOCTOR – Preciso de um médico

POLICE – Polícia

I'M LOST – Estou perdido/a (use "perdido" if you're male, "perdida" if you're female)

IT'S AN EMERGENCY – É uma emergência

GLOSSARY

ACQUITTAL: A jury verdict that a criminal defendant is not guilty, or the finding of a judge that the evidence cannot support a conviction.

ADVERSARY PROCEEDING: A lawsuit arising from a controversy that begins with filing a complaint.

AFFIDAVIT: A written statement made under oath.

APPEAL: A request made after a trial court has decided against one party in which the losing party asks a higher court to review the decision for legal error.

ARRAIGNMENT: A proceeding in which a criminal defendant is brought to court, told of the charges, and asked to plead guilty or not guilty.

BAIL: The temporary release of a person from jail when awaiting trial, on condition that a sum of money be lodged or deposited to guarantee an appearance in court.

BARRISTER: A lawyer admitted to plead at the Bar and who may try cases in superior court.

BURDEN OF PROOF: The duty to prove disputed facts.

CAUSE OF ACTION: A legal claim in a civil action.

COMPLAINT: A written statement that begins a civil lawsuit in which the plaintiff details the claims.

CONTRACT: An agreement between two or more persons to do something or to not do something.

CONVICTION: A judgment of guilt against a person charged with a crime.

CUSTOMS DUTY: A tariff or tax imposed on goods when transported across international borders.

COURT LIAISON: A person that coordinates with attorneys to perform administrative duties, such as scheduling witnesses, sharing information with law enforcement, and overseeing the reporting of cases to foreign embassies when applicable.

DAMAGES: Money that a defendant pays to a plaintiff in a civil case if the plaintiff wins.

DEFENDANT: 1) The individual against whom a civil claim is filed; 2) The individual against whom a criminal claim is filed.

FELONY: A serious crime, punishable by more than one year in prison.

MAGISTRATE: A judicial officer of a district court, who conducts initial proceedings in criminal cases, decides criminal misdemeanor cases, conducts many pretrial civil and criminal matters on behalf of district judges, and decides civil cases with the consent of the parties.

MISDEMEANOR: An offense punishable by one year or less in jail.

PLAINTIFF: A person or business that files a formal complaint with the court.

PLEA: In a criminal case, the answer of "guilty," "not guilty," or "no contest" in response to a criminal charge.

SOLICITOR: A lawyer who advises clients, represents them in lower court, and prepares cases for barristers to try in higher courts.

SOVEREIGN IMMUNITY: A legal doctrine by which the sovereign or the state (i.e. government) cannot commit a legal wrong and thus, it is immune from criminal and civil liability and cannot be sued.

STATUTE: A written law passed by a legislative body.

STATUTE OF LIMITATIONS: A statute prescribing a period of limitation to bring certain types of legal actions. If the action is not brought within that time, the person or entity (in a criminal context) is permanently barred from suing in court.

SUBPOENA: A command, issued under court authority, for a witness to appear and to give testimony.

TESTIMONY: Evidence presented orally by witnesses.

VERDICT: The decision of a judge or jury in a case.

WARRANT: Court authorization to conduct a search or to make an arrest.

ACKNOWLEDGMENTS

This book series would never have seen the light of day without the able assistance of the following people:

Kathy Adams, my paralegal for over 22 years, who is the "Best" I've ever worked with during my entire legal career because of her amazing work ethic, organizational skills, and her ability to think outside of the box in unique and creative ways;

Ally Knez-Siddique, a professional writer, and one of my paralegals, whose eye for detail, according to her, is both a blessing and a curse;

Gino Ibanez, my former law clerk, whose exceptional research skills helped move this book series along in its early stages;

Rosa Diaz Graham, my legal assistant who helped with research and word processing at the very beginning of this project;

Shelia Martin, one of my former paralegals, worked diligently on this series of books, even after taking on another job. Her organizational skills are reflected throughout;

Mindy Scarlett, my marketing and publishing "Guru"! Her creativity and vision have no boundaries!

ABOUT THE AUTHOR

Michael L. Moore practices in Orlando, Florida, the city where he spent his formative years. He credits the trauma of having his brother murdered when he was only 10 years old, as the catalyst that drew him into the practice of law.

Moore attended Florida State University, where he was a member of the FSU debate team. Upon graduating, he was awarded a full scholarship to attend the University of Tennessee College of Law, where he was elected President of the Student Bar Association. He further honed his advocacy and public speaking skills by participating in 'moot court' competitions.

After clerking at the Tennessee Attorney General's office while in law school, Moore moved back to Orlando, Florida, to work at the State Attorney's Office as a prosecutor, and where he was fortunate enough to meet the young lady that would eventually become his wife. Moore moved on to working for private law firms, both local and national, and eventually established his own law firm in 1999. He continues to make Orlando his home base.

It was the murder of a close friend and client in Jamaica that caused Moore to realize that books on laws in other countries were few and far between, and he was inspired to create Law of the Land Publishing. Moore launched Law of the Land Publishing to provide a series of guidebooks and a membership site for tourists and business travelers to stay up to date on the laws in each country they travel to, as well as having access to assistance if they run into legal issues.

"My vision is to educate people on what their legal rights are, and how they can access legal assistance, no matter where they have to travel to in the world," said Moore. "As Americans, we have a right to due process, but in some countries, you don't even have the right to access a square meal when incarcerated. My goal is to provide the information needed to stay out of trouble, as well as having access to assistance if trouble finds you."